"A gift from Marianne's heart to yours – life's lessons told with love, humor, and spirit. Marianne captures us with her stories and makes us pay attention to the sacred messages of everyday life. There is not a mother who won't relate to her trials and learn from her wisdom."

—Debby Peoples, C.S.W., Coauthor
Experiencing Infertility

"In *The Sacred Weave of Mothering*, Marianne Franzese Chasen takes us on an intimate tour of the potential of family life! She has written a beautiful book that eloquently describes her own growth and development as she tends lovingly to the growth and development of her children. Her wisdom, passion and patience are perhaps the greatest ingredients for a very necessary kind of social activism. This charming book will serve as a recipe for change in our troubled world."

—Joanna Lerman, Ph.D., Director,
The Parent and Educator Forum, Huntington, N.Y.

"Marianne illuminates the dark corners of mothering and then inspires a way out with hope and grace."

—Kim Sarasohn, C.S.W., Psychotherapist,
Private Practice, New York City

"Thank you, Marianne, for reminding me and everyone who reads your heartfelt book that love can't be measured in the way that we measure things. Your message to trust that the act of receiving expands our capacity to love and to be loved is one that we must hear over and over. *The Sacred Weave of Mothering* empowers us to trust the truth."

—Susan D. Astor, M.S., Founder of Playorena®,
Coauthor, *Gymboree: Giving Your Child
Physical, Mental and Social Confidence Through Play*

Dear Shari —

To a truly
soulful woman!

May the road
ahead hold
many blessings.

Warmest Wishes,

Marianne

The Sacred Weave of Mothering

Reflections...
from the Depths of the Soul
to the Heights of the Laundry Pile

Marianne Franzese Chasen

Aslan
PUBLISHING

Fairfield, CT

Aslan Publishing
2490 Black Rock Turnpike, #342
Fairfield, CT 06432
Please contact the publisher for a free catalog.
Phone: **203/372-0300**
Fax: **203/374-4766**
www.aslanpublishing.com

IMPORTANT NOTE TO READERS:

The examples in this book relating to personal and relationship growth and effective parenting are not meant to substitute for the advice of a trained professional such as a psychologist or psychiatrist. The publishers and author expressly disclaim any liability for injuries resulting from use by readers of the methods contained herein.

Library of Congress Cataloging-in-Publication Data

Chasen, Marianne Franzese, 1962-
   The sacred weave of mothering : reflections-- from the depths of the
soul to the heights of the laundry pile / Marianne Franzese Chasen.
      p. cm.
   ISBN 0-944031-91-9 (pbk.)
   1. Mothers. 2. Mother and child. I. Title.

HQ759 .C485 2002
306.874'3--dc21

Editing and book design by Dianne Schilling
Cover design by Miggs Burroughs
Photography by Nicki O'Connell
Printing by Baker Johnson, Inc.
Printed in the USA

This book is dedicated to
my four loves—Emma, Lili, Sage and Mary—
I pray that I will be able to raise you above my imperfections...

...and to Lee,
this is my song to you.

Acknowledgements

My heart feels so happy to have the opportunity to name the many people who have made this book possible.

My thanks must start with my parents, Mary and Luigi Franzese. As an adult I can now appreciate the passion and dedication with which they raised their children. Both my mother and father have taught me so much about living life in a soulful way. I want to honor the love with which my mother received the words of this text. I am so grateful to have my parents, my father in spirit, my mother in life.

I thank my three siblings, Paula, Rosalie and Louis for being the God-given refuge of my childhood and the chosen sanctuary of my adulthood. A special thanks to Rosalie for entertaining my children so I could write.

I thank my mother-in-law and father-in-law, Louise Chasen and Arthur Chasen, for supporting me fully in my endeavor to move this book out of my kitchen and into the world. I thank my sister-in-law Leslie for her friendship and excellent advice on my manuscript.

I thank my nieces and nephews, Gregory, Daniel, Rebecca, Michael, Nina and little Louie for giving me the pleasure of being their aunt. I thank all my family members for gracing my life with the wonderful stories of our time.

I thank Jacqueline Dubbs Siroka for providing me with a pathway of empathetic communication. She gave me the key to my children's hearts. I will be forever grateful. I thank Judith Gleason for unlocking my voice. She provided a home for my words and trained me to write from my heart. I will never forget her teaching.

I thank Beverly, Bobbie, Sharon, Lenore, Lee and Denise for helping me to channel the ray of love and wisdom directly into my life. I thank Elaine Resnick for guiding me in meditations that helped me to expand throughout this process.

I thank Debby Peoples and The Women's Project for the summer writing group. It was there that the idea to write the Sacred Weave was born.

I thank my friends for contributing to the pages of this book by being compassionate witnesses to my life. Kim Sarasohn for the many pilgrimages we have made to the depths of our souls. Robin Schulman for her steady stream of comfort and support. Joanie O'Connor for the pleasure of our enlightening bus stop chats. Janet Zaslow for her zestful confidence in me. Celeste Carlin for her soothing reassurance and for arranging the publishing circle on my behalf. Diana Duchowny for the young girl poems that still resonate in my heart. Anne Silver for her resilience in navigating the rough waters of life. These women help me to be a better mother.

I thank my three powerpuff girls, Marygrace Berberian, Rosemarie Taliercio and Maura Griffin, for each in her own way saving the world before bedtime. I thank Alice Bruno for the love with which she cares for my children when I'm at work. This means everything to me. I thank all the clients I have worked with throughout the years for allowing me to see the beauty of their truth.

I thank publishers Hal and Barbara Levine of Aslan Publishing. Barbara's phone call telling me that she loved my manuscript will forever live in my heart. I thank editor and book designer Dianne Schilling, for asking wonderful questions in a kind way, and cover designer Miggs Burroughs for his keen eye and patience through numerous redesigns.

I thank Dan Monti for spending the time to photograph our family, and a special thanks to Nicki O'Connell of Bumblebabies in Bay Shore New York for her beautiful photography.

I thank everyone who allowed me to tell their story and for being part of my story. Diane Franzese, Micheline Taliercio, Colleen Taliercio, Rosalie Berberian, Patrick O'Connor, Gregg Cunningham, Kathleen Ruggeri, Kelly Markham, Craig Amarando, Camille Smith, Donna Anesolona Troisi. My prayerful thanks go to John Newton.

I thank my children, Emma, Lili, Sage and Mary for all the love and inspiration they give me everyday. This book is all because of them. I thank my husband Lee. We did this together. I may have written the words, but it is our union that made it possible. It is the mutual love and acceptance we share that gives us the miracle of our life together.

And of course, I thank God, with every breath I thank God.

Foreword

You're my mother,
You're my father,
You're my lover, my friend,
And I let you know cause you help me see,
To see who we are,
To see you in me.

I am in you and you're in me.
Come intensify,
Open up my heart and my mind.

I learned this song, sung by Fantuzi in the 1970s, while in spiritual training with Arika. It keeps playing in my mind as I read Marianne's book.

The oneness between mother and child after birth, and the desire to again experience this deep connection, influences our choices throughout life. Within the verses of this book, Marianne illuminates her journey of deep connection and it's impact on her roles as mother, friend, family and community member. Her reflections and memories are humorous and candid. Her words invite me to join her world and feel with her as she manages to sustain this intimate and sacred connection. I learn with her and her children about facing life's challenges and making everyday choices that can hold a higher vision.

Throughout this journey, the reader encounters mirrors where she can see herself as a "good enough" mother. Marianne allows us to reverse roles with her so that we may see and honor our own imperfections. Reading Marianne's book, I feel continually challenged and supported to be the best human I can be. I imagine that her children and ours will be less afraid to be in their own skin, and more able to risk being in deep connection, because of these words that she shares with us.

If you are hungry for connection, Marianne's book is food for the soul.

—Jacqueline Dubbs Siroka, ACSW
Psychotherapist
Director, Sociometric Institute, NYC

Contents

Introduction

The Sacred Weave of Mothering is a book of stories inspired by everyday life with my children. The messages I share come from a difficult labor. I've had to push past the image of who I thought I would be as a mother and give birth to who I actually am as a mother. In the process, I've been able to nurture my own authentic definition of what it means to be a good mother. As I have struggled over the years to grow more fully into the role, I have seen a miraculous transition occur in my family. Each day more of me becomes available to my children and, in turn, my children make themselves more available to me. In the home of acceptance, we meet each other face to face, heart to heart, and soul to soul.

I have written these stories from the truth of my soul. My decision to share them comes after much thought. It is hard to tell the truth. Yet I know that telling personal stories is one of the most profound ways to connect with other human beings. I have many feelings about having this book in the world. The strongest is a feeling of gratitude. It means a lot to me that you are letting my words into your life. My hope is that this book will serve as a faithful companion to you, meeting you wherever you are on your journey, shining light on the direction that your heart wishes to take, and reminding you of the lost truth that mothering is a most sacred art.

The sacred work of mothering requires a great deal of discipline and devotion. I never hit my children. I never shame them with words. I work hard to stay in close connection with each of them. Many times my anger has directed me to hit or shame or disconnect from my children, but I fight the desire to hurt with every conscious muscle in my body, and I am able to make another choice. It is possible.

We can make the higher choice when we take the time
to go within. In the space between the inner response and
the outer response lives the remembrance that our children
are sacred beings struggling to master the human experience. We serve as their guides and we must model what we
want them to learn. I want this book to support you in finding the courage and stamina to make the higher choices
whenever and wherever you can.

I offer my words to every mother who has dreamed of
becoming the Good Queen, but has somehow lost her glory
in the mirror of her children's growing needs. I suggest that
we sacrifice the image of who we think we should be and
replace it with the humble majesty of who we can be, based
on our individual values, strengths and passions. The identification and enhancement of our personal assets is so important, because they are the tools that we each bring to this
noble work. I want this book to empower you so that you
can embrace the intimate stories of your humanity. One of
the ways to take ownership of your crown is to honor the stories of your triumphs and defeats—past, present and future.

This book carries the metaphor of the weave. I chose
this metaphor because weaving is what the movement of
mothering feels like to me. From moment to moment I move
between what my children need to learn from me and what
I need to learn from them. It is in this dialogue that patterns
emerge and evolve into the fabric of our life. As the weaver,
I have the awesome responsibility for what is ultimately created. The threads that I speak of represent the individual
gifts that each of my children bring into my life.

The gifts, or threads, that our children bring are not
always apparent. Our most challenging children perhaps bring
the most sacred threads of all. I want this book to invoke a
reflective process from which you discover the threads of
enlightenment that your children carry. As you work with
the individual threads of your family, the doors of deeper

connection will open and the pathways between your souls will be sewn into place.

Every stitch of this book has been written to honor the authentic struggle of the soulful mother. The soulful mother doesn't always get it right. In fact, we make a lot of mistakes. But we hang in there. We search and we suffer and we wake up each morning with the promise to love our children better. We stand among our piles of laundry and sort through the ever-present concerns of our home and family. We dive into the turbulent waters of our emotions and we spin in the mysteries of ordinary life. We work and we worry and we wish that the failures of the day might be rinsed from our minds and bodies. We get tossed around from need to need and somehow we manage to generate the warmth of a mother's magic. We fold the clean clothes of the hour as we watch our children unfold the fabrics of eternity. We put away our desire to be perfect and we wear our love for our children without pretense. This book is written for all of us.

As we weave our stories together, I hold the faith that the common threads of our experience will once again inspire reverence for the sacred art of mothering.

Chapter 1
Threads

I have been given a task.

Four sacred threads have been placed in my hands.

A thread of Hope,

A thread of Truth,

A thread of Faith,

A thread of Courage.

From these four threads

I have been asked to weave a pattern of love

That combines the wisdom of the old way

And the beauty of the new.

The work feels overwhelming,

The process encouraging,

The outcome unknown.

I am scared.

Ties of Truth

From the moment I found out I was pregnant with my first child, I felt deeply humbled by the opportunity ahead of me. I knew then, as I know now, that being a mother holds the potential for tremendous spiritual growth. The act of mothering is a challenging and precise art, which pushes me to bring the full breath of my spirit into everyday life. It takes great care to spin the different color threads of connection between each child and me. I am a mother to four children. I have three daughters and one son. I feel blessed. I feel exhausted.

Most of the time, my days with my children are very mundane. We eat, we dress, we shop, we clean, we play, we do homework and we hurry from place to place. There are moments, though, when I make the effort to slow down to the point of stillness, and the ordinary suddenly becomes a vision of truth. It is then that my soul is filled with the knowledge that to be a mother, and to be fully present as a mother—emotionally, spiritually and physically—is to be at one with my own divinity. It is then that I feel grateful—deeply touched—that these precious souls have chosen me to be their mother, to teach, love and protect. To provide home, the inner and outer foundation of safety, in which they can take root.

I have given myself the challenge of approaching my day-to-day encounters with my children in the most spontaneous and loving way possible. By spontaneous I mean choosing new and appropriate responses to the behaviors at hand based on the information I receive from my mind, body and soul.

Sometimes I fail miserably at meeting my challenge. I lose my focus and get tangled up in a knotted mess. At the end of those days I feel terrible. I think. I cry. I promise to do better tomorrow. I remember, I am a human mother. I can hurt and I can heal. I convince myself that never making a mistake is not in the best interest of my children. True or not, it helps me to feel better.

I love my children and yet I know it is inevitable that I will disappoint them. I am learning to live with the fact that I will make mistakes, because I trust my promise that I will acknowledge and take responsibility for my choices. There are times, however, when I am at one with my challenge. It is then that the act of mothering is transformed into an art and I feel alive and inspired in the role.

My commitment to spontaneity is really a commitment to the creative force within me. In order to keep the purity of the silken threads, I must comb through my own issues and clear them in a space separate from my children. I need to reflect upon the material that we create on a daily basis with people who understand and support my quest.

It is my connection to the love I receive from Lee, my husband, father of my children, partner and friend, that allows me to put my vision of motherhood into practice.

Together we spend time gathering the materials we need to build our love.

Together we create our very own wheel of life.

Together we are more.

It is my connection to the support I receive from the women in my life—mother, sister, aunt, cousin, friend—which allows me to accept the range of feelings that come up in being with my children.

Together we sit at our benches and spin our stories.

Together we take our momentary breaks from the work of our life.

Together we breathe.

It is my connection to the guidance I receive from God, which allows me to stay aligned with my soul's purpose in being a mother.

Together we generate the force that moves the wheel.

Together we spin the threads of loving connection.

Together we create opportunity.

The transformation of each thread

Through its connection to another is

The miracle of this sacred art.

The Courage to Walk

No camera to capture the moment,
No videotape to record the event,
My eyes focus through the lens of my soul
On little legs learning to walk.

Holding on to the coffee table,
The walk-around is safe.
A sippy cup across the room. . .
Down on all fours
Or attempt to officially join
The Clan of the Two-Legged?

The moment has arrived,
The choice is unsteady.
Let go with one hand,
Then the other,
Balance is tentative.

Standing on two legs
Without holding on,
A little garden statue,
Stone-still in my living room.
The attempt to step is filled with thought,
Cemented in the knowledge of the impending fall.

The risk locked in the eyes
Is released with complete abandon
As the initial step is made.
The momentum of breaking free
Fills the body,
Accelerating the speed of each new step.

One.
Two.
Three, four, five.
Six, seven, eight, nine, ten.

I hold my breath knowing that the fall is about to come.
I dare not interrupt the rhythm of new legs
Discovering their power to move through the world
In a way that allows everything to be seen differently.

Balance is lost.
The triumph over fear remains,
Illuminating a little face that is surprisingly relaxed
And completely satisfied with the tiny distance traveled.

Time and time again, in my daily life as a mother, I retrieve this moment from the archives of my soul. I remember the courage it takes to learn to walk a new path. I remember that once the first step is made, the other steps can follow quickly. I remember that walking and falling are surprisingly more relaxing than standing stone still, cemented in fear.

I am just learning to walk the walk of motherhood. When I can remember that, my days become at once difficult and easy, and I can be completely satisfied with even the tiniest distance traveled.

Initiation of Hope

Three years old.

The time has come for my youngest to use the potty. After almost ten years of changing diapers, I can see the end in sight. One more child to train and I'm done.

I'm ready. She's ready. We're both excited. And so begins her initiation into the mysterious world of toileting.

Sixteen pairs of new undies decorated with Power Puff Girls, Winnie the Pooh, and Blues Clues sit neatly in her drawer. A new potty seat with Big Bird, Elmo and Cookie Monster cheers her on. A big jar of M&M's with all the colors, including the new purple ones, is waiting on the counter to toast her success. Two sisters and one brother line up at the bathroom door with books and games, eager to keep her company.

All systems are go!

She changes her mind.

She wants her diapers back, but the door has already been opened, the threshold already crossed. There can be no turning back.

I forge forward, put her on the potty, and sit on the bathroom floor. I coach her, hour after hour—nothing. I run the water. Nothing. She says, "Nothing has to come out."

I say, "You are in charge of your body."

She gets off and pees on the living room floor.

I keep at it, day after day, accident after accident. She talks about it, she just doesn't do it. I start to worry. I ask Lee, "Do you think something is wrong with her bladder?"

"No Marianne, she is just learning."

"The other kids learned so quickly. Do you think she's a little slow?"

"No, training takes time. She's fine."

I give her time, lots of time.

She drags me into the bathroom. "Sit with me, Mommy, don't leave me." I won't leave her.

"Come on, you can do it," I encourage her. "Take a nice deep breath. Relax and push. That's a good girl."

Lee calls from the kitchen, "How's it doing in the labor room?"

Mary answers, "Nothing has to come out."

I say, "You know your body best."

She gets off and poops in her Dragon Tales undies.

Frustrated, I want to quit. I'm sick of cleaning up the mess. I just want to leave her in the living room with her poop and her pee, forever. I yell, "You are supposed to make on the potty."

I grab the jar of untouched M&Ms and lock myself in the bathroom. I want to go back to diapers. I wish we'd never started.

I force myself to find some hope in all of this. I flash back to my oldest child's kindergarten orientation. The reading teacher stands up and says, "Your children will face many struggles in their lives. Some will pass quickly, others will last longer. Your job is to hang in there with them for the long run."

I hear a little hand knocking on the bathroom door. She says, "I'm so, so sorry Mommy, I really am." I open the door and suddenly I am willing to hang in for as long as it takes.

Time after time, she calls, "Mom come in the bathroom and close the door."

I kneel in front of her and she looks directly into my eyes, allowing me to be completely with her. Our breath is joined.

Then one day it starts to happen. We both hear it. I don't say a word, don't move a muscle. I hold her eyes in mine as she finally surrenders to the call of her body. I recognize the moment as one of initiation. The door has been opened, she has crossed the threshold, there is not turning back. When she is done we both jump for joy.

One week later we plan a Potty Party to celebrate our freedom from diapers. We serve lemonade and chocolate ice cream, and sing silly potty songs.

My friend, Kim, is over. In a quiet moment she says, "It seems like mothers have to endure so many little losses to help their children move toward independence."

I'm too thrilled with our potty success to really feel what Kim is saying. It hits me a few days later when I walk into the bathroom where my little girl is on the potty, and she immediately insists, "Get out, Mom, I need my privacy."

I retreat.

She yells, "Close the door."

I stand on the other side of the closed door and ask, "Do you heed any help?"

She answers, "No, Mom, I can do it myself."

I say, "OK, great."

She says, "Now go away, Mom."

I try to step away, but can't. How did there get to be a door between us—me and the diapers, suddenly disposable? I stand still as a tingle of grief runs down my spine.

Hearing her flush, I run. She opens the door and emerges proudly. My hope is restored.

Awakened to Faith

My babies were not good sleepers. For the first few months after they were born, we loved hearing their little calls in the middle of the night. We loved feeding our infants in our bed with the blue glow of the soundless TV lighting their smiling, grateful eyes. By the time our first child turned one, we thought we should try the "cry it out" method. The book said that all it takes is three nights of crying and then the baby will be trained to sleep through the night. Lee thought the idea made sense, so we gave it a shot. I listened to my baby cry for five, six, seven minutes and then I was done.

I said, "This is crazy!"

Lee said, "give it another three minutes."

"What? I'm supposed to deny my motherly instinct to go to my crying baby because some male doctor says so? No."

"These things take time."

"It's time to be with our baby. I'm not letting her cry for another second. I'm just not."

"Marianne, you're setting yourself up for years of sleepless nights."

"So be it."

And so it was. With baby after baby, toddler after toddler, we were up during the night. During years of musical beds, we were never quite sure where any of us would wake up in the morning.

At first we moved through our days in a sleep-deprived fog, drinking coffee and eating sugar to create momentary bursts of energy. In time, our bodies adjusted and we somehow found a way to function on very little sleep.

In the dark hours of the night, a young cry would rip me from my dreams. Once the cry was answered, my body wanted to return to sleep, but my thoughts had already been awakened and the mystical space between my child and me had quickly filled with worry. The only way I found peace was to saturate the space with prayer. It was the first time in my life that I felt like I really needed God. My own mortality suddenly stood before me and living took on a new purpose.

My children awakened in me the need to pray. As a mother, there were so many things I had to be aware of and so many things I couldn't control. I spent many nights asking God for help, asking for guidance, asking for the protection of my children.

As the nights turned into years, my prayers began to change. I stopped asking and I began receiving. Slowly, I allowed faith to rest in me.

We saw that each of our children was ready to make it through the night in their own bed by the age of three, and we helped them to get there. Now our bed has once again become our own. At night I dream. In the day, I live with the presence of prayer all around me.

Chapter 2
Tools

The threads of
Hope, Truth, Faith, Courage
Summon the tools within,
Requiring the use of
My Body,
My Word,
My Vision,
My Presence.
I resist working with these tools.
They are not sharp enough
To meet the demands of these threads.
This work is bigger than me.
I am reluctant.

Showing Up

When I turned six my mother threw me a big party with all my new kindergarten friends. The day of the party I sat in my room and cried. My older sister, Paula, who was not quite eight at the time and who loved planning big theme birthday parties for herself, came into the bedroom and asked me why I was crying. I said, "I don't want to go to my birthday party. I'm scared of having so many people here just because of me."

Paula looked at me directly and with all her big sister authority, said, "You are the Birthday Queen and you are going to your party. It is the only way to get to be the next age. Family and friends make it happen. They get you to grow up."

I trusted my older sister and I showed up. I wasn't comfortable, but I showed up in my crown and I ended up getting a lot of really great gifts.

Twenty-two years later I sat in my room crying about almost the same thing. I had just started graduate school and the director of my program was hosting a party for all the students in the department. I was scared to go. I didn't know anybody and the thought of trying to mingle felt unbearable. I called my dad, who was in the hospital suffering from emphysema. In his Italian way he advised me, "Marianne, for a smart girl, for real, you are stupid. Go to the party. Who knows who might be there. And if you don't like it, stay ten minutes and then leave. That's all."

I listened to my father and I went to the party. I masked my anxiety with makeup, a pretty dress and a new haircut that made me look like an artichoke head. Still, I showed up. As I stood there in all my discomfort, my eyes caught a ray of light that traveled through the crowd. Across the room my eyes found Lee. He saw me. The reunion was instantaneous and joyful. We have been together ever since.

I realized then that all I need to do is
Show up
Every day
At the center of my life,
Counting on my family and friends
To straighten my crown,
To tell me when I need a new hairdo
And to nudge me on my way.

I finally trust that if I show up truthfully
I will be graced by the gifts that God intends for me.

Dream

*I had a dream during the early part of my pregnancy
with my first child.*

It actually felt more like a vision.

It was frightening,

It was comforting.

I dreamed that I had given birth to a dead baby.

*I was grieving quietly in a hospital room and my hus-
band entered.*

*He said, "You feel the fire of a mother's love. Your child
has died.*

To ease the pain, you are being offered a great gift.

You need to make a choice."

He brought in three baby animals.

*He said, "You can mother this baby whale as your own
child*

*And in your life it will take you to the depths of the
ocean*

And reveal the mysteries of our beginnings."

I said, "It moves so gracefully."

He then put the whale aside and brought me an eagle.

*He said, "You can mother this baby eagle as your own
child*

And in your life it will take you to great heights

And reveal the freedom of flight."

I said, "It has the kindest eyes I have ever seen."

He then put the eagle aside and brought me a lion.

He said, "You can mother this baby lion as your own
child

And in your life it will walk beside you and reveal your
connection to the earth."

I said, without hesitation, "I choose the lion cub."

My husband asked, "Are you sure?

"The others are becoming extinct and we may not have
this opportunity with them again."

I said, "I am sure.

"I cannot cradle the whale or the eagle in my arms.

"I can hold the cub.

"We can walk together upon the earth and we can share
the same home."

He smiled and handed me the cub.

I held my baby lion in my arms and a feeling of peace
filled my soul.

Then I woke up.

I treasure that dream.

It marked the beginning of the integration of my spiritual and physical natures.

$Born$

Before having children, my body was a temple of shame. I rejected and hid my legs because they were too fat. My breasts were too small. My arms were too flabby, my hips too wide. It was so uncomfortable to be in my body that I resided predominantly in the realm of my mind. I developed a very ethereal presence, which kept my hate for my body well hidden. Rather than allow myself to fully participate in the human experience, I moved through this earthly plane of existence like a spirit.

When I found out I was pregnant with my first child, I was surprised. It didn't seem possible that my body, which felt so dead, could actually produce new life. I got scared—really scared. I was sure that my body would betray me, as I had betrayed my body for so many years, and either destroy the developing fetus or create a baby with grave deformities. I actually felt embarrassed to tell people that I was pregnant. I felt publicly exposed as a physical being and I did not trust the life-giving power of my female body.

Though I liked to think of myself as an earthly woman, in fact I wasn't very grounded at all. In facing that truth it became clear that the way to find my connection to the earth was through the life force in my body. I stayed with my fears until they began to transform. I started to trust that I was in fact a fertile woman and that the child growing within me was indeed a child of the earth.

When I went to the obstetrician for the first time, I met with a doctor who was about to retire. He had been in practice for over forty years and, as an elder, had a common-sense wisdom about him that put me immediately at ease. As he examined me, he said, "Your hips are wide, that's good. Your baby will have plenty of room to grow. Your thighs are long and big—that makes for an easy labor. Your body-type is ideal for childbearing." In that moment I actually felt a shift in my thinking, and the shape of my hips and legs took on a whole new meaning. I played his words over in my mind and they became the foundation of a body concept that is based in pride rather than shame. After my initial visit, I never saw that doctor again, but his healing words had taken root.

I spent the summer of my pregnancy in bare feet. My husband would tease, "Look at you, barefoot, pregnant and in the kitchen." I would laugh because that image was no longer one of oppression or entrapment for me. As I lived it, I felt great freedom in my rootedness. It was a simple time when doing ordinary things brought me great satisfaction. The more I felt life within, the more I wanted to stay in my body. I began to experience the world through my senses and for the first time in my life felt deeply connected to my earthly heritage.

I drew great strength from my own mother's pride in her ability to carry and birth children—an area of life in which she truly honors herself. As I connected to that part of my mother that lives in me, I was able to nourish myself with the richness of self-love. I also felt part of a larger family—a lineage of Italian peasant women who worked the fields in their bare feet. That summer I ate a lot of Italian bread, fresh mozzarella cheese and ripe figs. In the afternoons I would take a siesta. Sometimes I would nap and other times I would just sit and watch my basil grow. It was a period of gestation.

As I came to the end of my pregnancy, I felt sad about having to let this state of being go. I thought that once I gave birth I would lose what had taken me a lifetime to find—an appreciation and respect for my body. When I went into labor and it came time to push, all I could say was, "I can't. I can't. I can't."

The nurses and doctor were insistent. "Honey you have to push. We can't do this without you. Come on now, push through the pain."

I held on and cried, "I can't. I just can't do it. It hurts too much."

My husband took my face in his hands and said very slowly, "Marianne, it is not a matter of can't. It is happening. You can either fight your body or work with it." His words cut through my hysteria and touched my heart as words of truth often have the power to do. He then said, "All your energy is going out the top of your head. Pull it down into your belly."

A nurse pushed him out of the way at that point and started yelling something at me. I don't know what she said and it doesn't matter because I had already received the coaching I needed and I was there, fully in my body, and able to ride the waves of my contractions and push with the force of my animal nature.

Three pushes later, my daughter had arrived and so had I. There we were, the two of us fully in our own separate bodies and both of us really hungry.

Word Matters

Three Years Old—

Still not talking.

My mother takes me to the doctor.

"Is something wrong with her?"

The doctor asks me,

"Do you know your name?"

Of course I know my name,

I know a lot of other words too.

I don't speak any of them.

I feel protective—my words belong to me.

11ᵗʰ Grade Religion Class—

A course called "Reflections"

Sister Mary Rose asks,

"When you die, what do you want to be remembered
* as?"*

We go round in a circle.

When it's my turn I say,

"As someone who took the time to listen."

The girls in the class laugh at me.

I feel ashamed,

My words are diminished.

College Major: Theatre—

I take on many different roles,

I study voice,

I learn how to project my words,
I get good at the craft.
On stage the words come easy.
I step off the proscenium.
The illusion gone,
I feel lost.
My words are not my own.

Writing Group—
Judith reads us words,
Beautiful words,
Exotic poems and stories
That I can hardly make sense of.
She reads and then we write.
I don't know how to respond.
She tells me,
"Don't think, just listen to what is true for you and let
* your pen go."*
I write and read my words
Every Monday night
For seven years
To a group that sees me as a poet
And does not judge my voice.
I feel found.
My words are accepted.

Psychodrama Training—
Wednesday night group.

Jacquie directs me in the stories of my life,

Helping me to find my own words,

Then moving me to reverse roles in order to find the words of others.

She diligently guides me

From the point of vagueness to the point of clarity,

Allowing my babble to emerge into meaning.

Seven years and 800 training hours later

I finally become fluent in my native language.

I step out of the circle and into my life.

I feel understood.

My words are healing.

First Year of Marriage—

Committed to a man

Who has strong convictions

And the firm backing of his intellect,

My words seem small in comparison.

I believe him when he says

That he wants me to be fully in my power.

He challenges me to be in my truth,

I take on his challenge,

I use him to learn

How to fight fair with my words.

I punch through the silence of feeling misunderstood.

I speak up for myself,

I discard my need to be right,

I replace appropriate words with authentic words,

I allow loudness to fill the space between us,
The dissonance is uncomfortable.
It eventually breaks.
Both our voices come back into harmony.
I feel loved.
My words are defined.

The Celestine Group—
I sit among seven women,
All my elders.
We practice meditation,
We call in the light of the universe.
In communion with these soul sisters
I connect deeply to God within,
I become quiet enough to hear
The voice of inner guidance.
I incorporate the words into my colloquial speech.
I honor the message to bring
The sacred into the mundane.
I feel balanced.
My words are blessed.

Today—
I sit absorbed in these words,
Questioning their place,
Writing and rewriting,
My mind searching for an ending.
Mary,

My youngest child,

Not yet three years old,

Climbs up on my lap.

She holds my face between her two little hands.

She looks deep into my eyes.

She says,

"Speak to me Mom. Speak to me."

I give her my words without hesitation,

I feel complete,

My words matter.

Chapter 3
Lessons

I will never feel ready enough
To begin the weave.
I will never know enough
To feel ready.
If I think too long about this
I will quit before I ever begin.
If I try to plan out the pattern
I will be stopped by inadequacy.
I don't know how to begin.
I need lessons,
I need teachers.
I am willing to learn.

Song of Her Spirit

Emma is my oldest child. When she was still a toddler she began to understand on a very deep level the responsibility of choice. We always allowed her to choose her own clothing, but around the age of four that choice became very painful for her.

One morning I was sitting with her as she tried to find something to wear. Nothing seemed to satisfy her and she refused to take any of my suggestions. She would put something on, look in the mirror and then take it off, crying, "I don't look good."

In the midst of her tears and my own frustration, I asked her, "Emma what's going on? Why is this so hard for you?"

She answered with great sorrow in her voice, "If I don't look beautiful, nobody will love me."

Her statement stunned me. I felt guilty. (What had we done to give her that message?) And, at the same time I felt grateful that she could express her struggle clearly.

My husband and I had reassured her that we loved her for who she was, not because of what she wore. But what did that mean to a child who was just beginning to have a sense of her own autonomy?

The challenge for us as parents became how to convey to our daughter the depth of our love for her as a physical, emotional and spiritual human being. She needed to hear why we loved her. As I listened to Lee express so concretely and eloquently the many different reasons he loved her, I felt at a loss. In my heart I knew I loved her just because she existed, and it really was that simple.

But Emma was asking something different of me that morning. She was asking me to step back and see her as a person separate from me. As I looked at her, really looked at her, with tears still in her eyes, I saw that she was beginning to be born into herself, and I understood the vulnerability of that process. I felt the loss of her no longer being my baby and, at the same time, I honored the courage of her presence and the opportunity to coach her through the darkness.

In saying, "If I don't look beautiful, nobody will love me," she was touching on a very important truth: that the act of choice is an act of self-definition. As we begin to define ourselves more clearly, it is true that some people will love us, some people will hate us and some people will be indifferent. For me, learning to tolerate that truth has been a lifelong lesson, and it is only recently that I've come to grips with my inner "knowingness" in the choices I make.

To my child I said, "Emma, it is true that some people may not love the clothes you wear, but what is really important is that *you* love the clothes you choose and that *you* feel beautiful when you wear them. Pick clothes that make you feel happy, that make your body feel comfortable and that make your spirit sing."

What I was trying to do was help her adopt new criteria for the choice of her clothing, criteria connected to self-awareness and inner truth. It took about two weeks, with lots of crying and clothing changes, before she began to integrate these new criteria. Though she really challenged my patience during those two weeks, my message stayed clear and consistent. "I know you can make a good choice for yourself."

I really believed what I was saying to her, because I trust the process of growth and I know it does not come without struggle. Emma did not have enough life experience at that point to trust the process as I do. I see it as my job to stay vigilantly connected to the faith that she will move through the stages of development with the strong support of her father and me. I will hold this faith for her until she can hold it for herself.

I approached Emma's struggle with newfound focus. When she would get dressed in the morning, I would refrain from saying that she looked beautiful. Instead I would ask, "How do you feel about your choice this morning?"

Emma would usually answer, "I like it. I look beautiful." And I would say, "I'm really glad that you feel good about your choice."

I remember asking her, some months later, if she still thought that people would only love her if she looked beautiful. She said, "No. I don't think that anymore. Now I think that people love me because of my spirit." Emma spoke a new truth and I have made the sacred promise to voice it for her, should she ever forget it.

Emma did spend most of her fourth year choosing only black clothing to wear. I resisted my desire to buy her brightly colored holiday dresses. Actually, I did buy them and I even tried to coax her into wearing them, but when she refused I returned them. I resisted my impulse to analyze why she chose black. I eventually resisted getting caught up in the comments made by observers of her choice. I let her be and trusted that these were the clothes she needed to wear to express the song of her spirit.

Emma is now turning nine years old. Recently my mother took her shopping for school clothes. After returning from the mall, my mother said, "Emma is so sure about her choice of clothing. Her sense of style is really earthy—just like she is."

Emma continues to allow her spirit to sing.

Her Way Of Love

Lili is my second child. She was born when Emma was only fourteen months old.

Sometimes I feel such a surge of love for my children that I have to grab them and give them tons of little kisses and growl, "Oh, I love you so, so, so, so, so, so much." Then I release them from my clutches and we each go on with the doings of our lives.

I never really gave this primal, eat-you-all-up way of love much thought until the day my seven-year-old daughter, Lili, came to me and said, "No offense, Mom, but I don't like the way you love me."

Wow! The power of those words was enough to stop me in my dishwashing tracks. I took a deep breath, put my offense aside and entered the door she had opened for me.

"What do you mean?"

"Well, you just catch me, and squeeze me, and kiss me, and it hurts."

"I'm sorry, I didn't know that."

"I like the way Dad loves me better."

"Okay, how does he do it?"

"He opens his arms and says 'Come, let me hold you a little bit,' and then I come to him."

"I get it. You feel ready to be loved with Dad and I catch you off guard."

"Right and I don't like that."

"That's important for me to know because I really want you to be able to take in my love. When I grab you and kiss you, it feels good to me, but not to you and that's not right. My love should feel good to both of us."

"But sometimes your love feels right."

"Like when?"

"Like when you lay on my bed with me at night, or when you let me sit on your lap when you're having your coffee, or when you kiss me before I go to school."

"Those are the times you feel ready to be loved."

"Yes. I need to feel ready."

"Okay. I will really respect that about you from now on."

"Thanks Mom."

"So how about a gentle hug?"

"Okay."

We hug and she goes back to her puzzle book and I go back to my dirty dishes.

Ketchup disappearing off plates,

Fighting back tears,

I don't want her to see me cry.

Let the water run,

Let the tears go dry.

Not now,

Later.

After she goes to sleep

I'll talk about it with Lee.

I'll cry then.

I don't want her to misunderstand,

I don't want her to feel like her truth can hurt me,

Not now,

Not after she gave me a piece of the puzzle,

A key to unlock the love between us.

Wash away

These tears are mine.

They're not of her or because of her,

I will not let her take them on.

Tears of disappointment

That our love doesn't flow easily,

Tears of regret

That I didn't see the obvious,

Tears of resentment

That she can allow her father so much more room than she can allow me.

Warm water

And wrinkled hands.

I want to cry

For the miracle of her voice.

Seven years old,

Finding the words,

Trusting me to hear them,

Knowing there will be no retaliation,

A bridge is built and

Transcendence occurs.

I feel such a surge of love for her,

But I contain it.

I look over to her,

She looks up from her book and

We share a smile,

A simple, loving, sweet, little, knowing smile.

The tears are coming.

I turn off the water and

Head toward the laundry room.

I quicken my pace,

Throw the clothes in the dryer,

Grab the basket of my kids' dirty laundry and

Cry into their little shirts and little pants and underwear.

I hug and kiss and squeeze their dirty little clothes close to me.

They're still so little,

There's still time to love them right.

Mama's Boy

Sage is my third child. He is my only son.

My beautiful boy tries not to cry as he walks into his first day of pre-kindergarten. I peek through the window and catch a glimpse of his sweet face. He is sitting with his hands folded, nodding his head as the teacher reads a story.

My husband tells me I need to be careful because I tend to treat our son like a little Prince, jumping at his beck and call. I say, "Bullshit. I treat him no differently than the girls."

Lee realizes that he just entered a defensive zone and immediately he backs off. I, of course, am now ready to fight and won't let it go. But Lee, after nearly twenty years of being in relationship with me, knows better than to engage. I'm left to mumble curses at him about how he shouldn't start something that he's not willing to finish.

My sister-in-law, Diane, made the mistake of referring to my brother, Louis, as a Mama's Boy. She was pregnant at the time with their son, and so my mother heroically contained her words and simply stated, "Soon you will be a mother to a son and then you will know."

My cousin, Colleen, has three boys. Her oldest is nine. They all still call her Mama. She says she likes it that way.

My sister, Paula, talks about feeling such a sense of sadness every time she has to leave her son, Michael.

Sage, my wise old boy, says as he is getting out of the car, "Mom, you're the best mother I ever had."

I say, "I am? Why?"

He says, "Because you always treat me so, so nice."

Diane and Louis come over for a Labor Day barbecue. Their son is now six months old. He cries, Diane jumps. She jumps, he laughs. He laughs, she laughs. Their eyes sparkle with love.

Louis hasn't eaten yet. My mother makes him a plate. She gets him a fork, a glass of wine. She sits him down. "I made sausage and peppers especially for you." He eats. Her eyes smile to have him at her table again.

OK, maybe it is possible that I treat my son differently than my daughters. But what is the difference? It's not in the degree of love I feel. Maybe it's in the way that the love flows between us.

I blend with my girls. There is a sense of oneness in our love. We start out connected. The energy then moves us to find each other in our separate places. The work of our love is to acknowledge and accept each other as different people.

I start out separate from my son. There is a biological distance in our love. The energy then moves us to find each other in our places of connection. The work of our love is to build and maintain the bridge of our oneness.

Right now there is no one my son would rather be with than me. He is four years old, and I know that soon this will change. He'll jump off the sweet, flowery bridge we built and land in the arms of his father. They'll both roll around in a pile of dirt and then mark the territory leading into the World of Boys. I will be left standing there with the bouquet of yellow dandelion weeds he just picked for me.

Lee gets an inspiration for a new boy toy—a toddler doll called "Daddy's Boy." It will be a little boy who says, "Pick me up Daddy," and "Let's go play ball Daddy," and "Can I help you in the yard Daddy?"

I say, "Great idea but I have one suggestion. I think Daddy's Boy should also say, 'Isn't Mommy wonderful, Daddy?'"

Lee gets really snotty and snaps, "Sorry. I don't think so."

"Why not?" I challenge.

"Because can't Daddy have his own separate connection with his boy without having the Mommy sink her clutches in it?"

"Why can't the Mommy be integrated into the relationship with the Daddy?"

"Because this is the Daddy's Boy doll."

"So I guess there needs to be a Mama's Boy doll to balance it out."

"No. I think there are enough of those already."

"Oh my God, I can't believe you just said that. All boys start out so adoring of their mama, but then in order to enter a man's world they have to throw us away like a beat up old doll. You're just like the rest of them, Mr. Touchy-Feely-Daddy-Doll Man!"

"Marianne, no one is throwing you away. Boys just need time with their Dads."

"Don't you oversimplify this."

I'm disgusted. All I can think about is calling my friend, Kim. She is a psychoanalyst doing research on female psychology. She is the only person who can help me make sense of this dialogue.

I'm pulled out of my fuming, interior discourse by the sound of my little boy's voice yelling for me from the upstairs bathroom. "Mom, I'm ready."

I walk into the bathroom and see that he has built a magnificent structure out of my twenty-five rolls of Costco toilet paper and my pile of precious Oprah magazines.

"So what's this?" I ask.

Sitting on his throne, he proudly announces, "I built you a bridge, Mom, for when you have to come over and wipe me."

The Blessing of Enough

Mary is my fourth child and, just as each of my children has come with their own teaching, Mary came with the lesson of *enough*. When she was born, I knew that four would be enough. The calling in me to have more children was quieted.

As I pushed her into the world, I gave birth to my declaration of "Enough!"

Enough of the endless labor! Enough of the laundry, the diapers, the bottles, the sleepless nights, the diaper bag, the car seat, enough!

And as it usually goes in life, just because I was ready to declare "Enough," didn't mean my world was ready to hear it. I was now the mother of four young children. Their needs came first and the work became literally endless. So I adapted my declaration to, "I have had Enough of sacrificing in silence!" I gave myself permission to complain, and complaining really helped! I liked it. It made the labor feel less sacrificial and helped me to lower my expectation from doing it all beautifully to doing enough to get by.

Mary set the limit and I expanded. In being able to say, "I've done enough service for today," more of me became available for my children. My fear that there wouldn't be enough of me to go around was pushed aside. Mary took her place, opening a new chamber of love in my heart. As I moved into that sacred space with my four children, I knew that for the time being I would be closing the door to many of my other connections. We entered our own galaxy—me, the mother star with her four planets in constant revolution. It was what had to be and, somehow, Mary provided entitlement to be in this space without apology.

I can write about this now because Mary just turned two and is beginning to find her place separate from me. There has been a shift and I can feel the change. My children do not orbit so closely around me anymore. This gives me the momentary pause to notice where I've been and to recognize that even in our most static places we are in constant motion. It is this recognition that helps me to appreciate that the mundane blessings of each day are enough.

Mary has taught me that love is enough, and love can't be measured in the ways that we measure things. I knew Mary would be the last child born to me, and so I was in no rush for her to move through her babyhood. From the start there was mutual acceptance in our connection. I treasured her in all her stages of early development and she received with full satisfaction whatever I could give her. If I could hold her for fifteen minutes or five minutes, it was enough. If I could sing her four lullabies or one lullaby, it was enough.

The more she accepted me in my compromised capacity to be the perfect mother, the more present my love became. Again I was met with the paradoxical notion that the acceptance of limitation brings expansion.

Mary received my love fully, so I was able to give it fully. I was free from the thoughts that block connection—the chorus of guilt, the list of chores, the buzz of time ticking. There was no obligation in the flow of love between us.

Before Mary, I always thought of being the "good enough" mother as somehow putting my children in a situation where they had to settle for less. So I fought giving into being "good enough." I fought to be better than that. When Mary came I had no choice but to surrender to the defeat that I was going to be less than who I wanted to be in my role as mother. The miracle that Mary brought into my life is that, in allowing myself to be less, I in fact became more—more human, more soulful, more connected.

Today I continue to struggle with my criteria for "good enough." I find myself returning to the question, "Is this really good enough?" in just about all areas of my life except for one.

When a gesture of love is made to me, whether it is from my children or husband, friend or family member, I try to receive it with the purity of heart that Mary showed me. No matter how big or small the gesture may be, it is enough and I feel satisfied—not necessarily because my need has been met perfectly, but because I have come to trust that the act of receiving expands my capacity to love and be loved.

Now when friends and family see me in the daily labor of raising four children, they ask, "So, is four enough for you?" I answer with a smile of silent gratitude, "Yes. Four is enough for me."

Chapter 4
Weave of the Past

I have been handed the plans
Passed along from my mother to me.
I need to review the
Weaving patterns of my life,
Images jotted down in memory,
Symbols of what was real and what was felt
Coming together like notes on a scale.
Highs and lows
Creating the song of my soul,
Many of the verses forgotten.
My mother's chorus remains
The message weaving in and out,
Simple and clear.
I am loved.

Birthday

Mom,

I celebrate you today.

As mother and woman,

I carry you in my heart,

In my soul,

In my bones.

Your mothering has created

A very warm place in me

And from that place

My children have been born.

Thank you

For honoring my spirit

And recognizing my connection

To the Source of Goodness.

I celebrate you today,

I celebrate your history,

I celebrate your existence into the future,

Mother and child

Connected through time,

Connected in love.

Always, your daughter,

Blessed Mother

I carry with me a legacy of women
who were raised to quietly weep
at the foot of the cross.
The Good Mothers in my family
respected the laws of Honor.
They avoided the sin of speaking the secret dialectic,
The one that expressed the fullness of their truth,
With anyone but God.
The mother tongue was to be sacrificed on earth
As a way to become Blessed Mothers,
Mothers who could love deeply and endure much.
This humble teaching has served me.
As a mother I am often called upon to make sacrifices.
I can do it without resentment,
I understand the holiness of such an act.
I am grateful.

I kneel before the Virgin Mother,
I pray for an answer,
"Will I get in trouble for making my truth known?"
She answers immediately,
"Let me be your example."
I understand her suggestion.
The Blessed Mother is beginning to speak up and out.
She is making her truth known,
Appearing throughout the world,

Weeping openly.

I embrace her message of compassionate action,

I call upon her strength

To help me resurrect my voice.

I stumble over these words. I realize how difficult it is to speak this mystical language. I realize how loved I feel by those who can understand my words. It is a great act of love to hear and accept another person's truth. This is the legacy I want to pass on to my children, a legacy where the voice of truth is held to be sacred.

This is the Word of the Mother.

The Choice

When I was four years old I went into the hospital with a mysterious virus. I had a high fever and a strange rash. No matter what the doctors tried, they could not stabilize my condition. I heard the adults talking in serious tones and I saw my mother crying a lot, so I had the sense that I might be dying. At the time, the idea of dying didn't scare me. I believed that if I died, I would become one of God's angels, and I would help him take care of the children in heaven. Actually, I wanted very badly to become one of God's chosen children.

Life was difficult at four. My parents were trying to keep their restaurant alive. My dad's eyes carried the heaviness of a lost dream and my mother's eyes held the burden of being buried beneath the piles of mounting bills. I felt their darkness and I was lonely. My older sister had gone off to school, and my mornings were spent by our front window watching for her return. As I waited, my mind drifted off into the misty world between daydreams and reality—the place where I lived at four.

At the hospital my mother kept me company with home-made chicken soup, and beef tea, and compassionate stories about the other kids on the unit. Every day she washed me, curled my hair, and dressed me in a beautiful nightgown. I loved our time together and, though I was getting weaker, I felt happy. My father was busy at the restaurant so he couldn't visit me during the day, but he sometimes sent lifesaver candies with my mother.

One night, in the middle of the night, my dad came up to the hospital room. He woke me and said, "Listen carefully, you are very sick and if you don't start eating and making yourself better you will die. Either you choose to live or you choose to die. If you choose to live, you can help God's children on earth. If you choose to die, you need to know that you will break your mother's heart."

Without hesitation I said, "Then I want to live."

He said, "Good. Now eat some meat. It will make your blood strong again."

I took in the nourishment my dad gave me that night and within days all my symptoms disappeared. The doctors had no answer as to my rapid recovery. My mother called it a miracle.

My father's intervention was of a divine nature. He spoke to my soul. I heard his message and made a choice governed by the heart. I chose life, and I have found through the years that the more I allow my heart to direct my life, the more alive I feel.

Today, when faced with the pain of hearing my children say, "I hate you Mom!" I remember the choice of my childhood. For the time being they live for me, just as much as I live for them. I know who we are to each other and, with complete faith, I can forgive their lie and help them find the truth of their anger.

Duck Story

Sitting Duck

My mother is a good duck. She always kept us in line and led us knowingly down a path of beauty, where family and education were the primary stepping-stones. She made sure we had good food and a warm nest and the safety of a mother who was not afraid to fight to protect her children. She led the way and we all followed.

Every day, whenever she turned around to do a head count, to make sure we were all still there, I would catch the momentary look of terror in her eyes at the possibility that one of us might have strayed when she wasn't looking, a pain she would not be able to survive. Loss, the built-in risk of love, was too difficult to face head on. We all felt her vulnerability and we all took good care not to abandon her lead.

She lost her own mother just as she was about to test her wings. Deeply injured by the severed bond of an unconditional love, she grounded herself in the reality that, at eighteen years old, with both parents dead, she had to step into the lead and keep her siblings moving along the path to what came next, or stop and die from the pain. She would not be a sitting duck. She made a choice of courage. She packed up the inheritance of her mother's unconditional love in a little black box and carried it in her heart as she found her way through the darkness. The luxury of lingering in the seemingly endless love of a young mother's arms was over, her innocence buried.

I always knew there was a hidden place in my mother's heart, a door I could not open, subtle and well guarded. I stood on the outside and lived in the mystery of my mother's true nature. Whenever any of her children got too close to uncovering the tender earth beneath her dignified stance, she would retreat as if we had seen the hidden weakness of her motherhood.

Not understanding that it was in fact my mother's strength that was hidden behind the locked door, I vowed never to hurt her in a way that could expose the contents of her vulnerability. This vow became the black box that I carried in my heart. I thought it would protect my mother. In the short run, maybe it did. But in the long run, it deprived her of knowing the fullness of my true nature.

Here I am, nearly forty years old, with four kids of my own and somehow, in the midst of the chaos of my life, I happen to look over and see my mother playing with my children. Suddenly I realize she isn't guarding anything anymore. Her love is fully available and I am the one who now needs to free her from the black box of my childhood experience.

My mother spent a weekend with my older sister and her children in New Jersey. When I spoke to my mother about the visit she said, "I wish I had more time to be with Paula." When I spoke to Paula about the visit she said, "I found myself following Mommy around all weekend like I was a baby duck—just wanting to be close to her." We are still lining up behind my mother, looking at her back, even though she has turned around and is ready to face us head on.

My mother and I went at it head-on this summer. A simple misunderstanding at my house led to the words I dread hearing. "I'm never coming back here again."

Stunned by the terror of having lost her, I reached in and broke open the black box I had been securing my whole life. I yelled out my uncensored truth: "What do you mean you're never coming back here again? How can you say that?" Expecting she might crumble from my open display of annoyance, I stepped back and cried. My mother calmly turned around, looked me in the eyes and said, "That was wrong of me to say. Of course I'm coming back."

The door to her heart was not locked. It was revolving. Before my eyes, the pure innocence of my mother's love flew out and about and into my hands.

The next morning a baby duck found its way to my backyard. Abandoned by its mother, a fuzzy little critter alone in the world, willingly jumped from my husband's hand right into my living room.

My mother said, "His arrival is a sign of spirit. Pay attention to the message he brings."

Baby Duck

Okay,

An abandoned baby duck in my living room.

Up comes a cardboard box from the basement....

Newspaper,

Water,

Cheerios,

Four kids flapping their wings in joyous hysteria.

Our dog on the alert,

Holding,

Petting,

Peeping,

Begging,

Barking,

Chirping.

Can we keep him? Can he stay?

Phone calls,

Duck doody,

Paper towels,
Clorox bleach.
The dog poops in the playroom,
Oh no.
The local wildlife refuge is full,
They're all full.
Keep him,
Find his family,
Put him out to die.
Father duck and three of his ducklings
Go out to scan the waters of Babylon.
No match in the local waters.
Gail the Naturalist from Massapequa
Tells me they make very good pets.
I don't want another pet,
I don't like pets,
I don't like the smells,
And the feedings
And the clean ups
And the possible bugs and germs and diseases.
Pets make me cranky.
I love the image of the mother
Taking in strays with ease and compassion.
I'd love to be a mother like that,
But I'm not.
And again I am forced to stretch beyond who I am
To make room for a new life,
Another baby who would die if we turned away.

I can't love a duck,

But I can take care of him.

Down comes the playpen from the attic.

He needs a roomier home,

He needs a name.

I say Jo Jo,

The kids say Pip.

Pip it is.

I avoid holding him. Then I take my stand. I line up my four ducks, look them in the eyes and firmly announce, "I will feed and care for this bird only under the condition that you promise not to complain about what I feed you from now on." They all promise—with all their hearts.

That night when the kids go to bed, Pip paces his playpen peeping away. He needs a nest. I warm up a towel and an old tee shirt in the dryer, and crumble them together in the corner of his pen. I pick him up and, for the first time all day, I stop and look at him. He is such a vulnerable little guy—soft and confused and trusting. As he snuggles into my neck, I feel it happening. The gold and silver threads of light start spinning around us. The gift that God gives babies to form the connection to life, their helplessness transferred into the love of a mother. Suddenly it becomes safe to be alive. The connection complete—mysterious, delicate, imprinted. After a while I put him down in his little nest. He tucks in his head and goes to sleep. I can love a duck.

Over the next week, my kids seem to complain about their meals more than ever. Pip, on the other hand, loves his romaine lettuce and wet wasa cracker combination. So much for my big condition.

The condition of motherhood is colored by an element of helplessness. I have become so vulnerable since my children entered my life and yet I've had to become strong enough to lead them down the path of independence. Every day I nuzzle the secret truth that my children hold power over my heart. They can hurt me and still I love them. I stand on my superficial platforms and convey the conditions as to what my children need to do to retain my love. I do it in an attempt to feel more in control of a love that has a tremendous capacity for forgiveness.

Lucky Duck

I have always known that my mother loves me unconditionally. Most of my life I have been afraid to test her love because I haven't wanted to risk hurting her. As a result, I've been able to let her see and know only a small part of me. I do not want to be in conflict with her because she might die like her mother did, and we would be left unresolved. I try but I cannot heal the hurt my mother carried. No matter how good I am. It is the hurt that created the one condition on my mother's love. She has to be alive for me to receive it. The knowledge that mothers can die is the cross I helped my mother bear.

My daughter, Mary, is named after my mother. She is the baby of our family and she does not like the idea of a new duck in the house. She walks around saying, "The ducky misses his Mommy. He wants to go home to his family."

I possessively squawk back, "I'm his Mommy now. We're his family."

The television is on. Chucky from "The Rugrats" finds a baby duck. Pip hears the quacking on TV. He starts chirping wildly. Mary empathizes, "Oh, the ducky misses his Mommy."

Patrick and Joanie, our neighbors down the road, have a chicken coup in their backyard. We tell them about Pip. Patrick says he has a hen that has been sitting on her eggs for twenty-five days now and it doesn't look like they're going to hatch. He says he could sneak Pip in there and the hen would adopt him as her own. My kids are happy about the idea that Pip will have a bird mother. We all agree to give him over to Patrick's care. We keep him for one more night.

Here I sit

With my abandoned duck in one hand

And the jewel of my mother's love in the other.

The heirloom passed down

From my grandmother

To my mother

And now, after all these years,

I make myself available to receive it.

The condition is lifted,

My mother stayed alive through all the hurts

And surgeries

And losses,

And now she is ready

To indulge in the luxury

Of loving us, her children and grandchildren,

As if there is no tomorrow

And that scares me.

It makes me feel that if I let myself love her that way

She will die

And I will be left brokenhearted.

My inheritance,

The priceless imprint on my soul,

That a mother's love is a most sacred love,

The gift God gave the women in my family,

Now known to me, but still a mystery.

Our ability to imprint the mark of unconditional love
Is the true strength of my mother's line.

On Saturday morning, Lee and our four kids walk down to Patrick and Joanie's house with Pip and the leftover wasa crackers. I stay back. I'm not brave enough to watch him go. I love my duck, but I don't have to take care of him anymore. I look around my house. There's a ton of other things to take care of. I want to be brave enough to put everything else aside and luxuriate with my children in the love that we feel for each other, but the thought of being so alive makes me feel like I'm dying.

My mother calls. She wants to take us on vacation. I tell her to save her money. She says she wants her grandchildren to enjoy her money while she's alive to see it.

I remember my inheritance,

I tap into it.

The gold and silver threads begin to reproduce.

In the light I pay attention to the message.

My mother and I are face to face,

She is still alive to see and know more of me,

My kids are on their way home with the man I love

And I feel like one lucky duck.

Chapter 5
Weave of the Present

I see now that
Each day brings a new weave,
Plain and poetic.
Am I quick enough
To catch sight of the
Pattern of the moment?
Am I brave enough
To trust the beauty of the weave
Before it's completion?
Loose threads of preoccupation
Unravel the presence of mind,
Enough with the distraction,
I am ready.

Happening

It is the eve of Emma's fourth birthday. She is sitting on the couch with her father. I'm in the kitchen cleaning up. I hear her ask, "Daddy, what do I have to do to become four?"

I hear him answer, "Nothing honey, it is happening all by itself." I am stilled by the reminder that it is happening. Little by little, each day my children are growing and whether I choose to notice it or not, it is still happening. I'm not sure why, but this makes me cry.

Lee tells me that my sentimentality takes me out of the moment. He's right. From time to time I remove myself in order to take notice of the blessings I have been given. When I look in on my life from a more distant place I can appreciate the richness of my simple existence and I can also touch the sadness that this very moment will never be again. In making the conscious effort to notice the happenings, I begin to fill myself with the tiny treasures of my children's transformations. This helps to ease some of the pain I experience around the passing away of each age.

It is the morning of Emma's fourth birthday.

She wakes with delight.

"Today I am four years old!"

I ask, "Where did three go?"

She answers, "It's inside of me Mom."

True.

Once again I am stilled,

This time by the wisdom of her words.

She is three and two and one

And all the ages she is yet to become.

As her mother

I have been given the great opportunity
To be part of her unfolding.
What a cause for celebration.
I take notice of her today
On her fourth birthday,
Sitting on her bed in her favorite red nightgown.
I give her a big hug and breathe in how tightly
She hugs me back.
I am beginning to understand that
In the happenings of my ordinary life
God speaks to me.
I feel happy
That we can be so familiar with each other.

New Year's Eve

On the eve of the New Year our family gathers around lit candles. We say prayers of gratitude. We pray that we may see our dreams recognized. We send prayers of light into the universe for those who are suffering.

Lili, our five-year-old daughter, feels the pain of others so deeply that she often suffers with bellyaches. Lili begins to cry. She remembers a picture she saw in the newspaper of starving children in Africa. She sobs. We hold her. We tell her that she has a wonderful heart for caring so much.

She says, "No, you don't understand. I'm not crying because I feel sad for those children. I look at them and I feel scared, so scared that I want to kill them. That's why I'm crying."

I make a silent resolution to notice the direction of my fears in the New Year.

Lee asks her, "What are you scared they may do to you?"

"I don't know. That's why they're scary."

He continues, "What do you think they want from you?"

"Food."

He smiles, "So, you can take those big strong scary feelings and use them to kill those children, or you can use them to feed those children."

Resolved, she throws her arms around him and lets out a sigh of relief.

Stopped

Racing through the day's errands,

Next stop the library to return the kids' tapes.

How much time do I have before the girls get off the bus?

Will I have enough time to get to the dry cleaners?

I miss the light at the five-way intersection.

Shit!

Three minute wait,

Thoughts intersecting and time flying,

This light takes forever.

Stopped,

I adjust my rearview mirror

And there I find

The reflection of my four-year-old boy

Sitting in the back seat

Looking out the window,

Mouthing the words to the song playing on the radio.

"I'm like a bird, I'll only fly away."

His blue eyes in a dreamy place,

His body still,

He seems content to be exactly where he is.

No reason to move

My baby bird forever.

As I hold him in view

I know that forever is moments away.

The light will turn green

And the race will go on.
What happens if the next time I look
The boy sitting in the back seat
Is going off to college?
Oh, these long lights are painful.

Witness

The night the baby monitor spit at me,

I learned that no witness walks away untouched.

I love to listen to Mary as she lies in her crib

And lulls herself to sleep with songs and stories.

Tonight I turn on the baby monitor....

I hear strange sounds.

I get closer,

I turn up the volume,

I hear Mary recount, in her two-year-old words,

An argument that went on earlier in the day

Between her brother and sisters.

I hear her growl,

*"Stop that right now. I'm angry. Everybody's being
    mean to me. Don't be mean to me."*

I lean into the monitor.

She sticks out her tongue and spits in disgust, "Pluh!"

I step back.

I touch my check.

It's dry.

I wipe it off anyway.

I listen.

I hear the rhythm of Mary's sleep breath.

I never even gave it a second thought

That she was present during the

Tuesday Sibling Battle Bot.

I didn't notice her during the fight.

She was quiet.
We were screaming.
I didn't check in with her after the fight.
She was happy.
We were miserable.
I didn't take care of her.
She was untouched by the event.
The rest of us were wounded.
I go upstairs to check on her.
She's sleeping peacefully.
I want to pick her up and hold her,
Apologize for forgetting that she was there to absorb
The anger that had nothing to do with her.
Tonight, I heard the silent witness.
Tomorrow, I will use her words as a way to monitor
Those around me when things start getting out of control.
Right now I spit out the understanding that
No witness
Ever walks away
Untouched.

In the morning, I will let Mary know that I heard her.

Chapter 6
Thread of Hope

I must find a way to run this thread of hope
Through the weave.
It is my reminder that
A choice,
Guided by the clarity of higher thought,
Can change the direction of the
War pattern.
A stop in the furious movement
Allows the power of this sacred thread
To take hold.
Simply spoken,
I am sorry.

Mirror of Grace

Growing up, my mother liked to say proudly, "My children are my mirrors." I have come to understand the depth of information that can be found in the two-way mirror that exists between mother and child.

I am often called upon to be a mirror for my children. I either model behaviors for them, or reflect back their own behaviors. There are moments, however, when my children become mirrors for me. This is great when I am happy with what I see. My children's success becomes a reflection of my success and that is very comforting.

But what happens when our children are allowed and encouraged to be fully in *their* truth? How do we look into a mirror that has become a pathway to our inner darkness? Do we turn away from such truth, or do we become like the Wicked Queen in *Snow White* who, facing the truth, is driven to kill her daughter in order to regain a sense of worth and power?

The summer we took our daughters to Sesame Place, we decided to spend a night at a hotel. As we were getting ready for bed, our then two-and-a-half year old daughter started acting out. She refused to put on her pajamas. She ripped off the diaper we had just wrestled her into, took her sister's teddy and would not give it back. Quite a struggle began.

Initially, we tried to approach her behavior from a place of understanding. We knew she was tired, and in a new place, and that we had to ride through this transition with her. With the best of intentions, we went from being playful, to empathetic, to all-out threatening, and nothing seemed to settle her. At one point we were all screaming at her and at each other, and the whole scene was out of control. It was clear that whatever we were doing was not working.

I decided to try separating her from everyone. I took her into the bathroom where she continued to tantrum even more fiercely, now because she wanted to get out. I remained firm. I sat with her and said, "Once you calm down we can go back into the bedroom and try again."

She screamed even louder, "Let me out now."

I said, "You need to calm down first."

She cried, "No. Let me out now."

As this went on for a while, I felt my rage start to mount. I just wanted her to shut up, and I knew at this point there was no stopping her and there was nothing I could do to help. My impulse was to grab her and throw her out of our hotel room and into the hallway. When I heard myself actually threaten to do that, I stopped and made a choice. Instead of giving into my rage and totally losing control of myself, I surrendered. The desire to fly with my aggression was much more appealing than giving up the fight, but I forced myself to sit down on the toilet seat and retreat from battle.

I listened to the inner monologue at the root of my rage. I heard the piercing cries yell out, *How dare you make me feel so helpless after I have tried so hard to make it better for you. You think you are so powerful but I will show you. I am going to win this battle, little girl.*

I listened, and I saw that my feelings of helplessness and frustration had led me to a place of Righteous Rage. I do not like this Righteous Rage because it gives the false impression that I am somehow entitled to squash my children in order to restore my sense of power. No thanks!

At that realization, I decided to stop trying to contain my daughter in her tantrum. Instead, I needed to face the mirror she was holding before me and try to contain my *own* inner tantrum.

That evening it became clear to me that it is very shameful and scary to face my limitations. My feelings of helplessness carried me across a bridge into craziness where it felt like the only way out was through the rage. The act of engaging a war to regain a sense of power, through the sacrifice of my child, is an absolute defeat as far as I am concerned.

I had to find another way out of my helplessness. For me, it came from taking the time to connect to myself and acknowledge both the difficulty of the moment and the truth that I can not always help my children through their pain, and that does not necessarily have anything to do with who they are or what they are doing. It has to do with my own limitations.

My father used to say, "When you make a mistake, you have to face the mirror, and once you have done that nobody can make you feel ashamed." I looked into my daughter's mirror and I met my Wicked Queen with acceptance rather than hate. I understood her existence, and her power over me diminished. Once I faced that image, I was able to see my daughter again.

There before me stood my little girl, crying and yelling with her diaper half on and half off. I felt such empathy for her and yet I did not feel the need to say or do anything. I let myself simply be a compassionate presence—a mirror to the pain beneath her rage. I was with her and I was at ease. I had fully surrendered the need to control her experience. I was able to just be there with her. As I arrived at that place in me, she immediately stopped her screaming, crying and tantruming. As unbelievable as that sounds, she really did stop—all at once. She then looked at me and said, "Mommy, are you sad because I am crying so much?"

I did not want to say anything. I opened my arms to her and she came into my lap. As I held her, I shared my truth. "Mommy felt sad when you were crying so much because I did not know how to help you feel better."

She said, "I want to go home. I miss my dog, Kiowa."

I said, "It is scary to sleep in a new place, but how about if Mommy holds you until you fall asleep and when it's morning we'll go home."

She rested her head and fell asleep.

Something very powerful happened between us in that moment, which allowed for a profound transformation to take place. She intuitively sensed the difference in my presence and it became safe for her to connect with me. I was not going to control her, or kill her power, or stick her with the responsibility of making me feel better. I was simply there for her in an authentically compassionate way. When she looked into my face, she saw the reflection of her own sadness and longing to be in a more comfortable and familiar place. I think she really felt seen and understood and, perhaps most importantly, accepted in our silent connection.

This interaction with my daughter has deepened my belief that it is the presence of a love that holds no judgment that makes it safe for us to journey out of our isolation and into the arms of someone who can hold us. In so doing we create a sacred space where the mirror becomes a pathway to our inner grace.

Meatball Moment

I stab a meatball onto a fork,
Stick it in my daughter's face and
Launch into my meatball tirade—
"You are going to try one of these meatballs.
I made them especially for you,
Made them with turkey chop meat
Because you won't touch beef,
Made them because you said you would try one.
Now you say, No.
No?
You changed your mind?
It's too late,
I already made them.
Do you think I like making meatballs?
Mashing raw chop meat with my hands,
Rolling the meat into a hundred little balls,
Frying them up in splattery oil,
Stinking up my kitchen.
You said you would try it.
You need protein,
Now try it!!!!"

I stare at the end of the fork.
I see this cockeyed little turkey meatball
Staring back at me.
And then it happens,

My meatball moment.
My brain chopped up,
My feelings mashed together,
My sensibilities rolled into a hundred little balls,
My words dropped in hot oil,
Splattering all over everyone.
I have become a Meatball Terrorist.
My God, I didn't know I had this place in me.

Acknowledgment brings transformation.
I hold up my forked meatball like a torch.
I liberate myself with a declaration to my children,
"I am acting like a meatball head."
The kids burst out laughing.
I say, "Forget the meatballs.
We'll save them for dad and the dog."
My daughter says, "You know what Mom?
It won't kill me to try one of your meatballs."
I raise my eyebrows and say,
"I don't know about that—
These meatballs seem pretty dangerous to me."

To Hell and Back

The strep infection invaded my home last year. We administered course after course of antibiotics—with no prescription plan. Many hundreds of dollars later, we are still no closer to getting rid of it. New toothbrushes every week, towels washed daily, door knobs, counter tops, floors sprayed down with bleach, play dates restricted, sheets constantly changed, hands chapped from washing, two dogs tested for strep at sixty dollars a culture and still the kids test positive.

Our pediatrician writes out yet another prescription. He tells me about a condition that has been documented called *Strep Neurosis.* He explains that in homes where there has been recurrent strep, some mothers begin to display obsessive-compulsive behaviors in combating the infection.

Go to Hell!

I take the prescriptions and curse the inadequacies of Western medicine. As I'm leaving the office, he calls after me and says, "Next infection, we'll send them to a specialist and get their tonsils out."

Shut Up!

As the year progresses, my daughter begins to display neurological symptoms in connection to strep. Her behavior becomes oppositional; she shows signs of motor and vocal tics. We go to the specialist. He says research is underway on the connection between strep infection and neurological effects. He says that in such cases aggressive treatment of strep is encouraged. I get aggressive. I'll do whatever it takes to keep this infection out of her body.

I put all the kids on supplements to build their immune systems. Six pills every morning, they go to school queasy. I take them to the chiropractor, adjustments three times a week. I put them on a special diet, eliminate dairy, wheat, artificial colors, preservatives. I become immersed in my own Strep

Neurosis. A month later they are sick again. My rage is reinforced by this defeat. I can see that my rage is ineffective, but I am blind to the ways of diverting its path.

Desperate for an alternative, I make an appointment with a homeopathic doctor at $200 for the first visit. I want to know if he has the remedy to cure this. He says that in Chinese medicine when a child is sick they treat the mother.

Go to Hell!

I'm sick of the mother being blamed for everything that goes wrong in a child's life. I'm sick of having so much power and at the same time having no power at all. Although I don't say this out loud, he stops talking to me. He talks to my daughter. She tells him that her regular doctor seems disappointed when her strep test comes back negative because then he doesn't get to write out any prescriptions. The homeopath tells her that her own body holds the secret to eliminating strep and she must learn to listen to and trust the wisdom of her mind and body.

Shut Up!

We leave the office with a ten-page survey, including questions like, "How do you feel during a thunderstorm" and "What do you dream about?" It all feels like a crock of new-age shit. I ask my daughter what she thought of the visit. She says, "Well, he really didn't like you, Mom, but he liked me and I liked him. I think he can help us." I trust my daughter's instinct and so I am willing to give this an honest try.

I think about what he said. I make a decision to look at myself. I see that I have been following the infectious direction of strep and it has led me straight to hell. My helplessness has secured my place there, and my aggression and hostility have certainly not helped me to find my way out. My thinking shifts. I decide to shut up my nasty thoughts. I begin to practice the daily affirmation that my children's bodies hold the inner wisdom necessary to heal. I become less afraid. I begin to work on balancing my energy. I make the time to breath and meditate. I ask myself why it is that I get so scared every time my children are sick. I comb through my past. I find connections. Understanding eliminates more of the fear. I pray for the empowerment of our minds, bodies and spirits. I ask God specifically for the blessing of good health. I receive the blessing of knowledge and I am free at last from my self-inflicted Hell.

My daughter and I return to the homeopath. He gives us sulfur. The symptoms emerge. We ride it out. The symptoms subside. He describes our constitution as being fluid. He says it is the nature of the empathic to take on the ills of the world. He helps us think about the containment of our well-being. We both feel better.

Six months later she gets strep again. Antibiotics become necessary. We fill the prescription with a sense of purpose. I work to manage my worry. I ground myself and remember the direction of my fear. Fear fuels illness and illness thrives on the poison of the ineffective rage of helplessness.

I take a new line of defense. My power lies in knowing that I am bigger than the bacteria that infiltrated my psyche and my daughter's body. My children hold authority over their bodies. I support their quest for wellness by accepting my place as a therapeutic agent. I am available to take them to doctors, to pray for them, to get their medicines, to instill the confidence that their bodies contain the miraculous ability to heal. I make the decision to administer each dose of antibiotics with love.

I am beginning to understand the power I hold as a mother. I need to be well in order for my children to enjoy the gifts of a healthy mind, body and spirit. Whether I like this power or not, I must observe it, because when it goes unchecked life becomes hellish.

When my children are healthy, I am happy.

The Valley

She comes down from her room,

Sheepishly eats her dinner.

I ignore her.

I purposely talk to the other children,

I call them sweetheart and honey,

I walk past her,

I won't look at her,

I want her to feel the loss of me.

She pushed too far, too hard,

Relentlessly standing on her mistaken conviction

That I lied to her.

Unable to reason with her,

Attempt after attempt

To help her understand what happened,

Attempt after attempt

To empathize with her disappointment,

Attempt after attempt

To ground her in the reality that plans change,

Attempt after attempt

Knocked down

With dismissive tones

And dirty looks

And accusatory insults,

Over and over and over

Until I could take no more.

Marie, the clairvoyant from Milk and Sugar Café
Told me that my name is
Endless Patience.
Well, I discovered the place
Where my patience ends.
The seemingly eternal path
Stopped in the middle of nowhere
At the edge of a cliff,
And before I knew it
I was free-falling into the Valley of Revenge.
The wrath of the Good Mother ensued.
The child, exiled to her room
Until she could return to the table
In a civilized manner.
She was condemned for her unjust behavior
And given the sentence
Of living out the evening
Without her mother's love or attention.

Not a word spoken,
She sits on the couch
Quiet,
Sad.
She dare not look at me.
Good.
I want her to suffer.
I want her to know that if she treats me that way
She will lose me.

I show no interest as she tries to come near me.
I look the other way as she is about to speak.
She retreats,
I feel justified.
Entitled to my sadistic power over her,
I am right,
She is wrong.
She deserves to be treated this way.

Very nice, this Valley.
I am disgusted with this part of my nature,
But it is there,
It is real
And I'm not moving.

She approaches again.
In a whisper she questions,
Mom?
What!
I snap back at her.
I'm sorry, she whimpers,
I'm really sorry.
Well I'm not ready to accept your apology.
I feel done with you tonight,
Done.
Please, Mom. I was wrong.
I don't want to lose you.
Just get away from me.
She slinks back.

I get out the mop and the pine sol.
I clean the dreaded, filthy kitchen floor.
I slop on the water
And force myself
To begin my ascent.
I've got to climb my way back
Up the side of the mountain.
It's too easy to get stuck in the muddy terrain,
Dirty footprints
On terracotta tile.
I don't understand
How it gets so dirty so quickly.

She deserves it.
No she doesn't,
She is seven years old.
I am thirty-nine years old.
I can't use my love as a threat.
I can't let silence be the teacher.
I have to take the lead,
I have to open the dialogue,
I have to be bigger,
Stronger,
Wiser.
I have to restore the balance of power.

I grasp the edge,
Squeeze out my mop,
Pull myself over,

Stand on the slippery floor.
Carefully I walk across,
Hang my mop out to dry.
I call her over to me.
I want to lecture her.
I want to go on and on and on
About how wrong she is.
I sit myself down,
I lecture myself instead.
Keep it simple,
Make space to listen,
Speak the truth.

Your words hurt me.
And when you hurt me like that
You will lose me
For a little while.
But I will always come back.
Always.
I'm telling you this because it is true,
And I hope that you will not
Take advantage of me because of it.
I won't Mom. I'm sorry I hurt you.
What did you do with all that anger you were feeling?
I went upstairs and I took my anger and squashed it like
    a bug so I could come down and be with the family
    again.
Suddenly I shift.

I am beside her on the path.
I am no longer in front of her
Wagging my finger in her face,
Making sure she gets what she did wrong.
No longer needing her to understand my hurt,
I am interested in her process,
The part of her she had to kill in order to return to me.
I return to the elder position.
I take her hand.

Help me understand what made you so angry.

Restoration

My father threw plates around the dining room when he
  was angry.

My mother threw words,

Swords of truth

Slightly rusted from the years of tears.

The truth hurts.

As a kid I ran for cover.

The plates I could dodge,

The words I could not.

They cut right through me.

Critical words,

Leaving wounds of shame and guilt.

Scarred by the thought that the way I was

Somehow hurt my mother,

Hurt her so bad

That she might leave me,

Or never talk to me again.

I wronged her

By not carving out a proper place of honor

For a mother who deserved to be treated like a Queen.

I stood on the sharp edge of her silence,

Tiptoeing apologies around her icy barrier,

My heart internally pleading

To be let back into her warm, loving eyes.

I sat quietly

And waited it out,

Hiding in my fantasies,
Creating the pretense that
I did not need her love.
She always thawed out,
She always forgave,
She always returned to her humble place
Of kind and loyal servant.
I welcomed her return with
Gratitude and relief.
She was good again,
I was good again.

But I was not completely well.
I became susceptible to the epidemic of my generation,
A low-grade virus lodging in the base of the soul,
Weakening our capacity to love ourselves,
Making us vulnerable to the damage of undetected fear.
Treated with repeated courses of antibiotics
Rather than the simple remedy of acknowledgement.
The mothers of my time were
Trapped in a culture that scripted their words.
Overworked and underappreciated,
The jeweled mirrors of Donna Reed
Slipped out of their hands
And shattered at their children's feet.

My mother's truth was right.
The force behind it did not belong to me,
It belonged to a lifetime marked by being taken for granted.

If only she had not been expected to do the impossible,

She would have had the time to notice more.

Recognition could have mended the broken mirrors in our eyes

And we would have been able to look at each other

Without the fragmented reflection of unworthiness.

I spent a long time looking into and through the eyes of what was.

Tears of what could have been run red,

Bloody vision that breeds contempt

Rather than reverence

For the divine purpose in every struggle.

The truth hurts,

But I emerged

Holding words as sacred objects

Not to be handled thoughtlessly.

Today I embrace the freedom

To see beyond what was

And into the truth of what is.

The truth is that my mother is a Queen.

She can hurt and she can heal.

It is the complex nature of her being that makes her

A fierce and faithful leader.

She can serve the needy from a place of equality,

Bringing the spirit of nobility to the unworthy.

She is a Queen who could not take her place of entitlement

Without the army of anger behind her.

The other night as I was rushing around trying to get my kids' dinner on the table, listening to their complaints, trying to accommodate their needs, I flashed into the fantasy of flinging their dishes across the dining room and yelling, "Now eat that, you ungrateful brats!"

By the miracle of a spontaneous decision, I chose to use that aggression to forge my way through the dinner madness and into my seat at the head of the table. I took my place in an attempt to restore Royalty to the Role of Motherhood. I sat up straight, said a prayer of thanks, ate slowly and engaged each of my loyal subjects in dinner conversation.

The truth heals.

Today I told my husband that when we get the money from our mortgage refinancing, I'm buying myself a chair. A throne of my own to be put in the front room, where I can sit with the robe of sunlight upon my shoulders and write words of truth.

As I write these words,

Tears fill my eyes.

I can see how much I did

And still do

Need my mother's love.

Tears of gratitude run clear

For a mother

Who raised me above her imperfections

To be a patient and knowing Queen,

A Queen whose wounds have launched

A vigilant crusade against

Words that hurt children.

Chapter 7
Thread of Truth

I welcome the sacred threads of others
That provide lines of direction
Leading to discovery.
I bow my head to these tender truths,
Spun through the eyes of love.
Over time
These threads gather together
And form
A thick cord
That anchors
Inner knowing.
I am thankful.

School Age

As a mother I feel very blessed with the educational experiences my daughter has had so far at JFK Elementary School in West Babylon. My gratitude comes from the authentic classroom character that each of her teachers has worked to create. When I speak of classroom character, I am referring to the individual values that these teachers bring to their position of leadership.

Classroom character reflects one of the sacred truths of teaching. It is the space that is created between teacher and student, where messages are conveyed about who the child is as a learner. It is the moment-to-moment, nine-to-three implementation of character education that is occurring in every classroom every day. It is the spirit that permeates the classroom, and that spirit is a direct reflection of the teacher's own character.

When I think of the four teachers my daughter has had—Mrs. Camille Smith, Ms. Kelly Markham, Mr. Craig Amarando and Mrs. Kathleen Ruggeri—I can see four different and honorable aspects of character education at work in their classrooms. They each seem to operate from a core principle, based on who they are as human beings, that guides their interaction with the individual students and the class as a whole. The teachers never directly told me their character creeds but I could hear it in the way my child talked about school, the way she felt about going to school and the way she experienced herself as a learner.

In Mrs. Smith's kindergarten classroom my daughter was welcomed into the school system with the character-building directive, "There must be trust in the process of learning." Mrs. Smith made sure all the children felt comfortable with the newness of the classroom situation. She encouraged them to take the risks necessary to become good learners, and she embraced them as they made their first mistakes. As a result my daughter took in the message, "I can trust myself in this world of learning."

In Ms. Markham's room, my daughter lived every school day with the character-building directive, "There is room for love in the process of learning." Ms. Markham worked to find the unique gifts that the children brought to their learning, and then generously shared her view of their specialness. As a result my daughter took in the message, "I am lovable as a learner."

In Mr. Amarando's room, my daughter experienced the character-building directive, "There is a need for community in the process of learning." Mr. Amarando showed zero tolerance for nasty talk and competitive behaviors among his students, and gave them opportunities to experience the power of working together to achieve a common goal. He helped his students become part of a successful team. As a result my daughter took in the message, "I do not stand alone as a learner."

When my daughter began third grade in Mrs. Ruggeri's classroom, I asked her, "What do you think Mrs. Ruggeri wants the children in your class to know about what it takes to be a good learner?" She thought about it and then she said, "Mrs. Ruggeri really wants us to know that there is a time for hard work and a time for silliness." Throughout the school year, I saw that spirit emerging in my shy girl. She had always been a hard worker, but it was as if she had been given permission to bring more of herself— the playful part of her being—into the classroom. My daughter was really happy as she experienced this process of learning because more of her truth was able to unfold.

Why is it so important that our children develop the character traits of a good learner? It is important because life is an extension of the classroom and the classroom is an extension of life. The happiest, most successful people see themselves as lifetime learners. If we look at life's challenges as opportunities to learn, the children who have taken in the more positive lessons of classroom character will have the confidence and self-knowledge to take on those challenges. When my daughter is confronted with a problem in life, I want her to return to the heartfelt lessons her teachers have taught her about who she is as a learner.

Character education is happening every day in every classroom and, as parents and teachers, we must become aware of the kinds of messages we are sending our children in every encounter we have with them.

I am very excited about the learning opportunities ahead for my daughter, but I do not take it for granted that every teacher will provide positive messages. I make it my business to listen to the spoken and unspoken information my daughter brings home about the character of her classroom. In consciously reflecting these messages to my child, I join her teachers in setting a foundation of sacred truth in her soul of learning. When she encounters negative messages, which she inevitably will, I want her to remember that *she can trust herself*, that *she is lovable*, that *she never stands alone,* and that *there is a time for all things in her life.* If she should forget, I can remind her because I have been listening.

Post Script

After writing this piece, I submitted it to our school newsletter in hopes of beginning a regular column on character education. Our principal agreed to print it under the condition that I leave out the actual names of the teachers. When I questioned his stipulation, he explained that such identification could make his teaching staff feel uncomfortable. I was saddened by the reality that these four soulful teachers would have to remain anonymous because of a fear-based reaction. I couldn't bring myself to omit the names, and so the article was never printed.

As I look back on the stand I took, I ask myself why it was so important to me that the teachers' names be published. Wasn't articulating the message more important than naming the messenger? I have come to understand that my need to have the names published was rooted in the value I place on accountability and responsibility in character education.

I was able to recognize and acknowledge the four teachers mentioned because, as a mother, I made an effort to understand the place of goodness from which each operates. They are good teachers.

Are these four teachers unique? Yes. Is every teacher unique? I believe so. Then what is there to be afraid of? If a teacher has somehow forgotten the essential goodness that called him or her into this profession of service, then as partners in education we need to help that teacher remember, rather than request that our child not be put in the teacher's classroom. If there is nothing good to remember, then that teacher's place in our child's life needs to be seriously and directly questioned.

I could not allow the article to be printed with the names omitted. As with our most sacred and ancient teachings, the messenger embodies the message. I don't think we can honestly talk about one without the other. It is the individual encounter with the unique nature of the teacher that provides the child with information about who he or she is as a learner in this lifetime. Every teacher carries this sacred responsibility and must be accountable for it.

The sacred truth of teaching is that the soul of the teacher is in constant communion with the emerging character, spirit and soul of the child. Maybe it is too risky to acknowledge that truth, but until we do I don't think there can be a meaningful dialogue about character education in our schools.

For now, I continue to listen. My daughter just entered fourth grade and her teacher, Mrs. Anselona Troisi, is new to the school. Though she may stand on new legs, her character message is sturdy and direct. At her winter holiday party, I saw on every child's desk a poem honoring the opportunities for learning that come from accepting each other's differences. As the mother of a physically challenged child, Mrs. Anselona Troisi knows first hand the pain a child faces when differences are not embraced. For her fourth grade students, this becomes a powerful directive to look beyond what is different in order to find what is ultimately the same. As my daughter now puts it, "We may be different on the outside but in our souls we all feel the same feelings."

So, even though my article was never printed in the school newsletter, I still make it my business, every day, to count among my blessings the teachers of JFK.

Fat Mama

Eight-year-old girls,

Sitting at lunch

Talking about their weight.

Sixty pounds,

Fifty-six pounds,

Forty-one pounds,

Forty-one pounds?

You're kidding?

No, I swear.

Wow!

My third grade girl,

Seventy-seven pounds.

I'm so fat.

No you're not. You're fine.

I'm fat!

Honey, you just had your checkup. The doctor said you are two pounds above the average weight for a girl your height.

Susan is forty-one pounds.

No she's not.

Yes she is—she swore.

Your four-year-old brother is forty pounds. You need to be forty pounds to get out of a car seat.

I know Susan

She is not forty-one pounds.

Well everyone else is skinnier than me.

Listen, you go back and tell your friends
That you are all growing girls and that
In order for your bodies to make the necessary changes
To become women
You need some fat on you,
And that nobody should be trying to be
Forty pounds
In the middle of third grade.
And you can tell them that your
Fat Mama said so!
Mom! I am not going to say any of that.

The next day at three o'clock...
How did it go at lunch?
I told the girls what you said.
You did?
Well, in my own words.
What did you say?
I said that you said that
Forty-one pounds is an unhealthy weight for girls our
    age and that we need some fat on our bodies in order
    to grow.
Wow. What did they say?
They said, "Emma, don't believe your mother, don't you
    know that parents lie all the time?"
Oh my God. What did you say?
I said, "Maybe your parents lie, but my parents never lie
    to me."
And they said, "Even about Santa Claus?"

And I said, "Even about Santa Claus."

Oh thank you, God.

Thank you for giving me Lee

With his big fat commitment

To being truthful with our children.

Thank you for giving me the courage,

After days of battle,

To surrender to his insistence

That we tell our children that

It is the "Spirit" of Santa Claus that blesses us each season when we give to and receive from the people we love.

Thank you for giving me the strength to respond to their demanding,

Sometimes tantruming,

WHY NOT?

With the God's honest truth,

Instead of giving into the temptation to say

The candy machine is broken honey.

Thank you for the confirmation that

Feeding my children a little dose of heartfelt truth every day

Lightens the load.

Mom? Ma? Mom?

Yes?

What's the matter with you?

I am just so fat with pride at this moment that I think

I'm going to burst.

Mom!

I am so proud of you for bringing the truth to your friends.

And I am So proud of mommy and daddy for never lying to you.

I still think I'm fat.

Well, we all carry an extra pound or two in this family,

But none of us carry the heaviness of lies.

Mom, you are so corny.

I love you...

All seventy-seven pounds of you.

And I love you Mom...

All one hundred and how many pounds are you again?

In Law

My father loved the law. He was an Italian immigrant who treasured the American Justice System. As kids, if we had a dispute to settle, or an appeal to make for a raise in our allowance, we had to schedule a hearing. On Sunday, my father's only day off from work, court was in session around our dining room table. My father served as judge, my older sister and younger brother as lawyers, my younger sister as jury, me as court stenographer and my mother as the Supreme Court of Appeals. We argued our cases, and laws were made in the spirit of fairness to the well-being of our family system. I loved when my family came together in the pursuit of truth. The power of that experience allowed the strands of love, law and family to be woven into a tight braid that ran down my back, creating the spine of my existence.

I get married. Suddenly I have a whole new set of relatives. I take on a family-in-law, a mother-in-law, a sister-in-law, a brother-in-law, a father-in-law, a bunch of aunts-in-law and cousins-in-law and uncles-in-law. Wow. There are a lot of new people to love. For me, love, law and family are already intertwined, so the transition seems easy. My husband says that we are lucky to love each other's families so much. I agree. I also know that it's more than luck. My in-laws and Lee's in-laws work hard to uphold the foundations of truth, justice and our family way.

On our wedding video my mother-in-law says, "Lee was so selfish before he met Marianne. She has been a gift to all of us." On the same video my mother says, "Lee, you must have done something very good in your life to deserve my Marianne." When we watch it, Lee looks at me and shakes his head and I laugh out loud. We both know the truth of our connection, but the image suits me just fine.

We spend a day with my mother-in-law out on the East End of Long Island. We pick vegetables from the farm and

ride the Carousel in Greenport. We have an incredibly se-
rene day. There is one short conversation, however, in which
my mother-in-law calls Lee a blabbermouth.

Lee takes on the mantle of a thirty-year battle waged to
wipe out family secrecy. My mother-in-law seems fragile as
she tries to get through to her son. I step back. I see her. I
step in. I translate her truth into a language Lee can understand. "Your mother is so vulnerable. Her world has been
shaken and all she wants you to do is listen to her and not
repeat what she says. Can't you do that?" He steps down
from his platform. He treats her more kindly.

We spend a day out in Brooklyn with my mother. We
go to the Santa Rosalia feast on Eighteenth Avenue and then
go to my mother's house for an Italian barbecue. She spends
the weekend cooking lasagna, eggplant, fried chicken cut-
lets, meatballs, sausages and a couple of hamburgers and
frankfurters to throw on the grill. She invites the whole family—cousins, brothers, sisters, children and friends. It turns
out to be a great summer Sunday. We're all just sitting around
playing when Lee says, "It's amazing, at sixty-seven years
old your mother still makes it all look so easy."

In an instant I grow up. I step back. I see the lines on my
mother's face. I see the slowness in her step. I appreciate
her more deeply.

In law, we are given the opportunity to see with expanded vision. The process is designed to help us step back
so that the truth can be seen. My sister, Paula, is a law pro-
fessor and she is committed to bringing to each of her students the message that the law cannot be divorced from love.
In law, as in love, the pursuit is of truth and justice.

The truth is that Lee and I love our mothers-in-law, and
so we are able to see them with an expanded vision of compassion. The justice lies in the fact that, as son-in-law and
daughter-in-law, we honor our duty to reflect back the higher

vision of what is present. We work through the trials, lifting the veils of each other's historical blind spots. It is the spirit of this exchange that allows the moment to be judged with understanding, rather than righteousness. As a result, our mothers can be seen in respect to their age and goodness.

I think about the long braid that once ran freely down my back. Now my hair is thick with waves and layers and a neat braid is no longer possible, but the spirit of the weave lives on. We are blessed, in law, in love and in family.

Bubblegum Auntie

I hate bubblegum.

My kids always end up swallowing it

And that drives me crazy.

I imagine the chewed up gum

Lodged somewhere in their system,

Their body working endlessly

To break down the resilient little wad,

Only to have it remain stuck

Deep within their being.

I refuse to buy it,

But that doesn't mean they don't get it.

They have a Bubblegum Auntie

Who keeps them well supplied.

Bubblegum Aunties are the ones

Who haven't had their children yet.

Their pocketbooks are filled with quarters

To put in gumball machines

And mechanical horsy rides

And the claw games

At the entrance of every Friendly's restaurant

That end up eating at least fifty quarters

Before the kids win their throw-it-away-after-two-min-
utes stuffed animal.

But Bubblegum Aunties don't mind.

They are creatures of pure delight,

Incarnated to serve the desires

Of the precious young hearts in their clan.

Fairy Godmothers with hidden wings,

They activate the stardust in their kiddie's eyes,

They bring the magic of a purely unconditional love

To the lives of their special babies.

Zizi, my mother's sister, was my Bubblegum Auntie.

She lived with us until she got married.

I remember actually jumping for joy

When she came home from work every night.

She was a force of light in our lives.

My sister Rosalie is Bubblegum Auntie to my children.

They call her Roro,

She calls them Pookie, Booba, Boo and Chudgey.

They wait by the window when they know she is coming.

One morning at half past six

I find my four children huddled in the bathroom speaking in whispered tones.

"What's going on here?" I see they have the phone.

"Who were you talking to?"

"Nobody."

"Come on, tell me."

"Promise you won't get mad?"

"Tell me."

"We called Roro."

"It's not even seven, what were you doing calling her so early?"

"Roro doesn't care."

"What was so important?"

"Princess Diaries is opening today and we asked her if she would take us."

"What did she say?"

"She said she'd be here at twelve, take us to lunch first, and then the movies."

I call Rosalie.

"Sorry the kids woke you up."

"Are you kidding? Do you know what today is? Princess Diaries is opening. We've been dying to see this all summer. We've waited at least two months for this day."

I hang up the phone and say out loud, "What is wrong with my sister?"

My son overhears and marches up to me with his hands on his hips and says, "There is nothing wrong with Roro. She just loves us so so much !"

Oh, God Bless the Bubblegum Aunties.

Mysterious, ageless, funny beings,

They never tire of telling their young how much they are loved.

I know that Roro has given each of my children

An opinion of who they are that really matters,

A glowing opinion that sticks

Directly to the soul of their growing identity,

Creating a resilient, unbreakable bubble

Around the pure essence of their beauty.

That's one bubble

I won't pop.

Chapter 8
Thread of Faith

When there are no easy answers
To the questions placed on the loom,
I drop my head in my hands and
I open my heart to the sacred thread of faith.
It loops over and under
And in and out,
Forming an open knot
That keeps the cloth from falling apart
As I search my soul.
I am sad.

The Good Shepherd

Kiowa's legs were never great. Bear helped for a while—a new dog for her to train in the ways of our family. This summer Kiowa's hind legs just stopped working. She could no longer stand on her own.

Medication did not help. Open sores developed on her hips from dragging her body across the floor. Lee carried her outside and held her up three times a day so she could pee. Then he carried her back in, laid her down on her blanket, patted her head and whispered, "That's my good loving girl."

As I watched him tend to her, day after day without complaint, bit by bit the ways he had disappointed me over the last ten years seemed to disappear. When I was a girl my father once said to me, "If you want to know a man's true nature, listen to the way he speaks to children and watch the way he is with animals."

So, for all the anniversary cards Lee forgot to write, and all the birthday presents he chose not to buy for me, I was suddenly filled with the gift of his true nature.

The vet suggested we put Kiowa to sleep. That evening we seriously considered this choice. Lee laid down beside Kiowa and held her. I sat in front of her and looked deep into the eyes of my good dying dog.

I asked, "What do you want to do Kiowa?"

She answered, "I am waiting for your permission to go. I am no longer afraid."

Kiowa was so scared when she first came to us as a puppy. She was eight weeks old, we were twelve weeks married—the three of us so unsure, each lacking in the kind of trust that only a solid history can bring.

The vet said that Kiowa had separation anxiety disorder. Taken from her mother too young, adopted from the

North Shore Animal League, rescued from a puppy mill, a tan and brown fuzz ball, our dopey baby shepherd had one ear pointing up and the other pointing down. She was a timid being with bold markings around her eyes that called attention to her desperate gaze.

She needed to be loved.

The vet wrote out a prescription for Prozac. Lee laughed and threw it in the garbage. I retrieved it and was very tempted to fill it and divide it among the three of us.

I was a Brooklyn girl living in the suburbs for the first time. Lee was out of the house working evenings and weekends and I was scared to death of the quiet darkness. Kiowa, with her insane barking, running, jumping and skidding across the floor every time someone passed the house, made me feel safe. She became my Shepherd of Protection.

One year later our first baby arrived. I did not know how Kiowa would react. Of course I had to read an article—the one time I picked up the newspaper during my whole pregnancy—about a German Shepherd eating a newborn baby. We prepared for the possibility of giving Kiowa away if she showed even the slightest aggression towards our baby.

Emma was born and Kiowa became a mother. She would never have puppies of her own and so our children became her children. With each baby that was born, Kiowa lovingly stepped back and the desperation in her eyes gave way to the gentle embrace of her gaze.

Kiowa loved our babies perfectly, even when they pulled her tail and dumped her food and tried over and over again to make both her ears stand up at the same time. She loved each child every day in a way that no human ever could.

As I looked into her eyes on the evening of the choice, it occurred to me that she embodied the love of the Divine Mother. With that realization, I asked, "How can we let you go?"

She answered, "You can let me go with the knowledge that my passing marks the end of a cycle. The work of this decade has been to transcend fear in order to set a foundation of trust upon which to build a home and family furnished with the teachings of love and truth. That work is done. I am home.

"A new cycle will begin and your circle will get larger as you move into the world. Bear will be with you now. He is a good guide dog. He is ready."

The day we put Kiowa to sleep I came home and stood outside. I felt strangely alone. A divine love had passed out of my life. In her passing I became momentarily dislodged from my ordinary existence. I became a tiny being in a vast universe and before my eyes the intensity of the human experience crystallized.

In communion with Kiowa's spirit, I lifted one ear toward the heavens and I heard the directive, "No one need walk this earth alone. Bear is waiting. Take him out with you."

I turned to my house with a deep sadness in my heart. It was time to walk through the door of a new decade. I took a breath and for the next month there was but one prayer in my mind.

Thank you, Good Shepherd.

Thank you for your love and protection.

It was in Kiowa's absence that I began this writing.

A Mother Lost

When a mother dies,

The world goes quiet

And in a passing whisper

The breathless cries of a child

Can be heard.

June 13, 2001. It is the morning of Helene Cunningham's funeral. I take my daughter to school at half past nine. As we walk through the doors of JFK, I am struck by the stillness. The building seems empty. There are no children walking in the halls. There are no teachers making their way in or out of the office. There are no parents busily attending to the end-of-year festivities. We walk into the office. The telephones are quiet. The unfamiliar secretaries are quiet. Mr. Cunningham's office—quiet. As I sign my daughter into school, I feel my heart fill with the overwhelming emptiness around me.

I walk my daughter down the long hallway. There is a substitute teacher in every class. The rooms are all dark. The same video plays on each TV. Some children are watching, some drawing. No one is talking; no one is out of a seat. My daughter and I walk in silence. I kiss her goodbye and stand for a moment in reverence of a loss that is big enough to still the children.

I feel myself wrapped in the sadness that the children of JFK feel for a principal who respectfully let them in on his journey of pain and, now, loss. It all happened so quickly. His wife became ill and the children noticed their leader's absence. They asked questions. And even though Mr. Cunningham was immersed in his own grief he made the courageous choice to let the children know the truth.

He honored his connection to the children of his school and, in his choices, made them feel significant. He allowed the PTA to organize prayer services at the local church. He allowed the children to pray with him. He allowed them to see him cry at the possibility of losing someone dear to him. He allowed them to see the human face of authority. In so doing, he created a truthful space in which they could become children of compassion.

Today, on the morning of Helene Cunningham's funeral, the children respectfully sit in their darkened classrooms, in silence. I quietly step into this moment, recognizing its grace and fullness. I know, whether it be a matter of minutes or hours, soon everything will go back to the usual way. I walk in awe of the collective love and respect that echoes in the halls of JFK. I walk in gratitude that Mr. Cunningham is a strong enough leader to allow the children to see his vulnerability. I walk in the knowledge that as human beings we cannot take our lives for granted.

As I walk out the door I feel torn by the universal bond of motherhood. I cry for a mother who left her children too soon. And I pray. I pray for her children. I pray for her husband. I pray for her peace. And as I pray, I realize what a powerful and humble legacy Helene Cunningham left behind. For me, it is a legacy that reminds us how fragile the thread of life can be, and how sacred the time spent with those we love really is. I pray that once I put my keys in the ignition and drive into the trivial concerns of my everyday life, I will have the wisdom to remember the teaching I received from a woman I wish I had met.

Circling

When a child dies

A mother circles the verge of death

For the rest of her life.

March 22, 1965.

My cousin, Marianne, died at the age of four.

Cause of death: asphyxiation.

She choked on a piece of meat.

She was laughing at her brother.

She was running from the table.

She died on the way to the hospital.

No Heimlich maneuver back then.

Her mother held her.

Her mother helplessly pounded her back.

The breath of life was gone from her body.

Her pink cheeks were blue.

Her mother pleaded to a God who could not save her child.

That night Zizi Micheline became the mother of a dead daughter.

When you lose your husband you become a widow.

When you lose your parents you become an orphan.

When you lose your child you remain a mother,

And somehow you are left to figure out

How to keep your child close to you

When you no longer have her little body to hold onto.

She buried her in a little girl's coffin.

At home, Marianne's room waited for her to return.

China dolls standing on a shelf,

Smiling at a neatly made bed.

A still life reality of life after death.

Marianne's mother held her place in this world.

From there she made a weekly pilgrimage to her daughter's new world.

She took good care of Marianne's grave.

She pulled the weeds

And planted flowers

And made sure the blanket of grass

Upon her daughter's bed

Was always soft and green and beautiful.

Every week before leaving the cemetery,

Zizi Micheline went to the place where

Flowers from the most recent funerals were left.

She sifted through the pile

And filled her shopping bag with the flowers that seemed most alive.

She took the flowers home

And spent the rest of the afternoon

Making extraordinary centerpieces.

For years and years,

Whenever she came to our house

For a Sunday visit

Or a holiday celebration,

She arrived with one of her flower arrangements in her arms.

My parents always received them with loving praise

And then humbly placed her loss at the center of the table.

Zizi Micheline never spoke about the pain she carried,

But when she brought her flowers it was understood.

As the family gathered around the table

There was silent recognition of the child who was missing,

And that collective thought set off a circling.

It was as if a ring of support formed around Zizi Micheline.

As we sat facing budding flowers

On the verge of death,

Pink petals turning blue at the edges,

Clinging to their short stems,

We ate

And laughed

And remained rooted

In the stories of the moment.

And though on the verge,

She held onto her place in life,

Still a mother,

Still in relationship with her daughter,

Still willing to learn

How to live

Between both worlds.

Twin Towers

My father used to say that we come into this world alone and we leave this world alone. Now that I'm a mother I know firsthand that we are born into this world attached. The cord gets cut and we are given a name. We begin our separate journey of growing up, but we do not grow alone. We grow alongside each other—twin towers, connected through the invisible cord of love. If we live the life we were meant to live, then we leave this world as we came in—attached.

September 11, 2001. When the big beautiful tower of strength and elegance was hit, my heart froze. It was an accident. It will be okay. Somehow it will be okay. The smaller tower, standing beside it, looking over at it's wounded partner, suddenly seemed so vulnerable. Attacked from behind, flames burst through its chest and my heart melted. Oh my God, this is no accident. We are under attack.

The cords of my attachments become inflamed. I need to get in touch with my children. I need to talk to my mother. My mother works across the street from the trembling towers. The phone lines are flooded. I can't make a connection. I feel like I'm going to die. I have to go get my children.

My husband stops me. "Hold on. The kids are safe. Let's just see what's going on."

The belly of the smaller twin explodes in terror and I can feel the screams as it crumbles to its death. My heart breaks as I watch the remaining tower struggle to hold on to life after losing its mate. Devastated by the detachment, it falls to its knees and with its last breath it pleads, "God help us all."

I need my kids home. I call my sisters, my brother. I can't get through. My sister calls, "Have you heard from Mommy?"

"No"

"What do we do?"

I go to pick up my kids. The secretary routinely asks me why I'm taking them out of school. I snap, "Because I'm a neurotic mother and if the world is going to end today then I want my children with me. If we're going to die then I want us to die together."

She raises her eyebrows and says, "OK. Who are their teachers?"

I take my children home. We are together, my lifeline restored. I can breathe. My sister finds my mother. They walk over the Williamsburg Bridge together. They are home.

The need to connect continues to cry out from deep within the rubble of my soul. I call out to the attachments in my life, the friends and family whose love can pull me out from under the broken beams of my heart. We rescue each other through our communal grief and gratitude that we are still alive.

I gather my children. It is time to secure their foundation in truth and faith. My husband and I will serve as an accurate source of information for them.

"Daddy, I've never seen you cry before."

"Nothing this sad has ever happened in your lifetime before. This is a day your grandchildren will learn about."

We answer the questions that expose them to the dark side of humanity and then we light the torch of faith. We call their attention to the tremendous displays of love and courage that abound at this crossroad. Good will prevail over evil if we unite in love for each other, the nation, the world, and for the survival of humanity. We pray to God.

I remember when the twins first came to New York. I watched them move in. I looked for them every time I made my way in or out of the city. I had ties to them. I loved that they had each other. I loved that they could stand together and watch over the smaller buildings. I loved that they were not alone. There they stood every day, holding thousands of people with thousands of attachments and, in an instant, a force of evil carrying the signature of no name deliberately cut all the ties. It is too hard to be in this world alone.

My mother cries about what she witnessed. She says, "I was not scared to die. I just didn't want to die alone."

In a day I have aged greatly. I look at the skyline and all I can see are the towering eyes of an orphaned city. The luxury of our youth is gone. The playground is covered in ashes.

I stand among the mothers who quietly weep at the foot of this sacred burial ground. I stand among the rescue workers. I stand among my fellow Americans. I stand among our nation's leaders. I stand among the sages of the world. I stand among the dead. We are the Collective, our hearts and minds joined in the recovery of love and wisdom to a planet that needs to be reminded of the power of our attachment to the freedoms of truth and justice.

I stare at the ashes—the fragments of flesh and concrete, metal badges and diamond rings. I pray for transcendence. I call to the souls buried beneath and plead for their assistance in lighting the way to a world without fear. From the depths of the terror, the Phoenix begins to rise out of the ashes. It is a magnificent creature with a wingspan large enough to carry the blessed beings that died at the hands of hate directly into the arms of God. Through their ascension, the cords of our connections are restored. Our voices on Earth join with our voices in Heaven in the prayer to our Father. Thy will be done, on Earth as it is in Heaven.

These are the ties that will deliver us from evil.

Chapter 9
Thread of Courage

I have discovered a hidden spindle
Wrapped with strands of courage.
I never knew such thread was available to me
Until I began this sacred task.
Every day, in ways that are great and small,
I must move beyond my fears for the higher purpose of
Letting love guide my thoughts, words, actions.
It is this single strand that holds the power to
Pull in the other threads of hope, truth and faith
In order to weave the Flag of my Family,
Past,
Present,
Future.
I am becoming stronger.

Conversation with Sage

(Age four, in the car)

I love you, Mom.

I love you, Sage.

I know.

That's good that you know.

Why?

*Because knowing that you are loved helps you to grow
into a good person.*

Mom?

Yes.

Do bullies feel loved?

That's a great question.

Do they?

I think bullies mostly feel scared.

Are they scared that they're going to get hurt?

Right.

*And that makes them mad, so they have to hurt other
kids first.*

Right.

Mom?

Yes.

I see a whale.

A what?

A whale.

Where?

There.

Where?

In the clouds.

Oh, a whale in the clouds.

Did you see it Mom?

No, I missed it.

Oh, that's okay.

Sage?

Yes.

What made you ask me about bullies?

I don't want to be one when I grow up.

You won't.

How do you know?

Because I know you and you're too brave to be a bully.

But I'm scared to go to school.

You feel scared but you go anyway. And you don't hurt anyone while you're there. That's what makes you brave.

Mom?

Yes.

I see an eagle.

In the clouds?

No, in the sky.

Flying?

Yes. Did you see it?

No. I missed it.

Mom! You miss everything because you talk too much!

I do?

Yes. Now can we just be quiet and look at the sky?

Okay.

Thanks.

Warrior Heart

I.

My heart starts to beat
With force and fury
In response to an act
Of disrespect.
The drumming of my heart
Calls me to the center
Of the circle.
At the base
Of my soul
And I want desperately
To wound,
With Weapons of destruction,
But I honor the ancient way
Of the Warrior Heart.
I take my grounded pose,
I align my powers
Of mind, body and soul,
I activate the lightening in my eyes,
I breathe in deeply
And then
I thunder down
The crashing word,
STOP.

II.

There is little tolerance for disrespect in my house.

When my children cross the line they know it

And the consequences are written in stone.

*Sometimes my husband and I disagree where the line is
  drawn.*

His STOP tends to come much quicker than mine,

But we are of the same Warrior Clan and

We do consider it our sacred mission to teach our children

To honor their people,

Their objects,

Their world,

Their being.

We can't let them make a mockery of our Way,

And so, when they test the limits

I invoke my Warrior.

I raise my voice

With force and fury.

The tone of my words Stops their fall

And the cords of my Heart

Pull them back from the edge.

III.

I was initiated into the Way of the Warrior Heart

When my oldest daughter was about three years old.

I don't remember the details of our encounter.

*I know I was angry with her for treating her younger
  sister meanly.*

I put a STOP to her behavior and I also gave her a
consequence of some kind.

She was very upset that I wouldn't give her another
chance.

She was crying and screaming and she was really mad
at me.

I stood by my decision,

My Warrior was in place.

I sat down and offered her my lap.

She climbed up crying.

She cuddled close to me as she defiantly whimpered,
"You're the meanest Mommy in the world. I don't like
you anymore. You're so mean."

I rocked her as I said, "I know, it's really hard to learn a
new way."

The lesson taught

With Might and Mercy,

For me, this is a great remembrance.

Weaving Between

Faith and Fear

Emma starts kindergarten. I offer to drive her to school every day. She does not like the idea. She wants to ride the school bus. On the first day of school we stand at the bus stop and wait. The skies are gray and the bus is late. When it arrives, Emma marches on board and smiles at me from the window. I stand on the corner weaving back and forth between faith and fear. The thunderous cloud opens in my heart and I pray as I watch that bus pass me by. It is a moment I will never forget.

Emma is in third grade. She chooses to do a biography project on Rosa Parks. As part of her research I take her to a senior center in Wyandanch, where she interviews an eighty-three year old man named John Newton about his experiences with segregation. He wants to talk to her. He tells her that he grew up in the South and that when he was a little boy he had to walk three miles to school every day because the black children were not allowed to ride the school bus.

He speaks about a day when he was walking to school in the rain. A school bus slowed down next to him. He thought he was going to get a ride. Instead, the driver looked him in the face and drove away. John Newton looks at me and says, "I stood on the corner. The rain was coming down hard, but I couldn't move. Thunder. Lightening. It was scary watching that bus pass me by. It is a moment I will never forget." He turns to Emma with tears in his eyes and says, "I was so angry that day." He looks down and then he looks up and laughs as he says, "I'm still so angry about that day."

Anger and Pain

I stand on the Kindergarten corner, fighting back the tears. The anger at letting her go is twisted tightly around my spindle of pain. I want to chase after the bus, flag it down, force my way on at the next stop and scream, "It's not fair. I want to ride with you."

I want to grab her off the bus and cry, "I'm sorry. I'm not ready for this. Tomorrow. Tomorrow you can ride the school bus. Tomorrow I'll let you go."

I want to catch her before she gets too far away from me. I want to fight for those few extra minutes each morning to drive her to school. I turn toward my house. I force myself to take a step—just one, then two, then three.

...And with each step
I squash a little piece of my desire
To slash the tires
On a school bus
That opened the door
To a child's civil right
To ride into the world
On her own.

We leave the Wyandanch Senior Center in silence. We get in the car.

"Mom, John Newton is awesome."

"I know."

"The way he told his story made me feel so angry and so sad."

"What do you think he did with all the anger he felt?"

"I don't know."

"Did he blow up the bus company?"

"No. He said he joined the Civil Rights Movement with Martin Luther King Jr."

"Right. Martin Luther King Jr. taught a way to get anger out without hurting anybody or anything. Civil disobedience."

"I learned about that. He got all the people to march together."

"Yes."

. . . And with each step
They squashed a little piece
Of their desire
To slash the tires
On a school bus
That closed the door
To a child's civil right
To ride into the world
With others.

"It's like how our teachers are fighting for their contracts. They march around the high school sometimes, and every Friday they wear green shirts that say 'Contract Now'."

"Exactly."

"Mom, does it work?"

"What?"

"What Martin Luther King Jr. taught."

"Yes. I think it works."

"Then why is John Newton still angry?"

"He's still fighting the tears, Emma. He needs the anger to fight the tears."

Restriction and Permission

Everyone tells me life is going to get easier now that Emma is in full-day kindergarten. Life doesn't feel easier. At home, I busy myself with projects. I get a lot done. I think about my quiet little girl smiling in the window of the loud bus. It makes sense that she wants to ride with all the older kids. But letting her go on the school bus every day? Is this a safe choice? I am caught in the weave between my power to restrict or permit her choices.

I feel a knot tightening in the pit of my stomach. I have to let her ride. I take a deep breath. I am with her. OK. I am on to another project for now.

Emma makes her oral presentation as Rosa Parks and shows the video of John Newton to her third grade class. Her teacher takes the opportunity to expand on Emma's research and talks further with the children about the restrictive laws of segregation and the courage it took to fight for permission to integrate. Emma comes home excited about how her project was received.

"So Emma, what's the most important thing you learned from your project on Rosa Parks?"

"I learned that you have to have the courage to speak up when you think people are being treated unfairly."

"Is anybody in your life being treated unfairly?"

"The teachers. They've been waiting a long time to get their contract and the school year is almost over and they're still wearing their green shirts. I don't think that's fair."

"Why?"

"Mom, remember back in September when I asked you why the teachers were waiting for a contract, and you said because they wanted to get paid more money and their bosses didn't want to give it to them? I think they should get more money. All my teachers work really hard."

"Why do you think their bosses don't want to pay them more money?"

"Well, maybe because teachers work with kids, and their bosses don't think that kids are important."

"It would be really upsetting if that were the reason. You can check it out, you know."

"How?"

"You could write a letter."

"Who would I write to?"

"I'm not sure. Look at your school calendar. I think it lists the names of all the people on the Board of Education."

"Great. I'll do it. Maybe my letter will help the teachers."

Emma runs off with the confidence of having just completed a successful project, and the inspiration of having her teacher recognize and elaborate upon what she quietly stood up for in her choice of Rosa Parks. It makes sense that Emma would want to give something back. But letting her write to the President of the Board of Education? Is this a safe choice?

I feel the familiar knot tightening in the pit of my stomach. I have to let her ride. I take a deep breath. I am with her. OK. It's time to gear up for another project.

Clarity and Distortion

I head down to the bus stop early on the afternoon of the first day of kindergarten. There is another mother standing there. Her oldest child also started kindergarten today. We ask each other questions. Questions on top of questions, weaving through the mystical world of what is known and unknown, creating patterns of clarity. She begins to embody my answer. My inner shaking becomes calm. I do not stand alone.

Scandal in the third grade. Tuesday morning I get a call from our school secretary. She informs me of a noon meeting on Friday with our district superintendent to discuss Emma's letter.

The superintendent is a noble man in an awkward position. He needs to check out the Board's suspicion. The questions loom. Did we put Emma up to writing the letter? Did we write it for her? Is our child being used as a political pawn? Did her teacher somehow plant in our child's head the idea of writing such a letter? Did her teacher use her classroom to spread political propaganda? Questions, heavy with implications of immorality and illegality, pollute the space between us. Questions on top of questions, some unasked yet directly implied, creating patterns of distortion. I begin to embody my answer. I become unshakably calm. I know where I stand.

I answer with a resounding, NO.

The superintendent calls Emma's teacher. Out of respect for her thirty years of honorable service, he tells her that he will not dignify the situation by asking if she had any part in producing the letter. He knows her answer. She knows that he must answer to the Board. Out of respect for him, she responds with a professional, "No." She knew nothing of the letter.

Case Closed. Within a week Emma receives a letter from the Board of Education. The first thing she notices is that the letter is unsigned. Words without a signature do not stand up.

Arrival and Dismissal

Joanie and I stand together, anticipating the arrival of our kindergarteners. We are parallel threads, stretched to the limit. We hold tight to the frame of the post card that articulates arrival and dismissal times. The bus is late. It is to be expected on the first day. Our eyes focus on the corner. We continue to lace together the bits and pieces of information we have collected about our school's arrival and dismissal procedures. We speak about it again and again.

Days pass and I cannot let go of the hurt I feel for my idealistic third grade girl. The questioning of Emma's letter feels wrong. Lee reminds me, "Asking a question is never wrong. Good questions lead to dialogue. Dialogue allows for change."

Well if that's the case, they asked a bad question because there was no follow-up dialogue. They got their answer. "No, nothing was done wrong in the case of Emma's letter."

So why haven't they followed up with questions about what was done right? Why haven't they asked how her teacher and parents managed to build a frame of reference from which Emma held tight to her ideas and then articulated them in a plain and luxurious design?

The answers ring in my head. From day one of third grade, Emma's teacher gives her students the message that writing is a powerful vehicle for expressing thoughts, feelings and ideas. She gives her students the opportunity to write in many different genres. She values content and technique. Emma becomes a fluent and competent writer. Emma arrives at the source from which her writer's voice flows under the guidance of her teacher. This is what her teacher did right.

As for us, Emma's parents, it is our personal and professional passion to help children find a language of expression that is respectful, authentic and satisfying. For the eight years of Emma's life, we have been working to help her find her own voice—a voice that is truthful and meaningful and connected to her heart. Suggesting that she write a letter to the Board of Education is a natural extension of our family values. That's what we did right.

Oh, it can get so tiresome, listening to the pounding of my warrior heart as the words rise and fall throughout the course of the day.

Emma reads her letter from the Board of Education and says, "Mom, they sound like they're mad at me, like I did something wrong."

The written words are politically perfect, but the tone is unwelcoming and somewhat judgmental, and Emma feels it. I tell her that she has the option to write back and once again express her thoughts. She looks at me like I am crazy and says, "No way! They don't want to understand me. Nobody even signed the letter."

Dismissed! Standing on the corner in the rain, vulnerable and yet hopeful, they slow down their political bus and then drive right past her, leaving her silent, as they remain anonymous.

Oh, the pounding gets stronger. The call to speak gets louder. The cloth in my head gets longer.

Our children need leaders—elders in the community who are willing to put their political interests aside and make room for a child to feel understood. Rage sets down its roots in the child who feels unheard, unseen, misunderstood. I am living in a district where a letter is sent home saying that a first grader threatened to blow up the school. I am living in a district where a student writes a comic book depicting the murder of another student. I am living with an eight-year-old girl who, after taking her strong feelings and expressing them in a respectful letter to the appropriate authorities, is left feeling dismissed.

Emma takes the letter and files it in the box of work that she is saving from the third grade. She doesn't speak of it again.

Violence and Radiance

My kindergarten girl is on her way home. We see Bus 18 approaching. Eighteen is the number of life. I feel so happy to see that big old yellow bus. I just want to hug it. I think of the violent feelings I had toward it this morning. I say, "Sorry Bus. Thank you for bringing my little girl home."

The weave loosens and I can breath again. The doors open. Emma runs down the steps and into my arms. She is radiant. I wrap her in the changing fabric of our love. She is home. I can rest.

I need to speak on behalf of my third grader. I need to meet the Board of Education face to face. It is easy to feel violent toward a group when the individuals have no faces or names. I want to bring shame to the West Babylon Board of Education. I want to call Newsday or News 12 and tell the story of Emma's letter. I want to take the letters and give them to the Teachers Association. I want to cause trouble. I want to stand up at a Board of Education meeting and point my finger in their faces and make them feel small. I want satisfaction.

I don't want to be eighty-three years old and still angry about this covert injustice. I am being called to action. I need to speak. The Board meets every other week. I am ready. My sword is in hand. I can't wait to go in and slice their talking heads off.

I'm not ready. I need to breath and loosen the weave. This is not the message I want to send. I must choose my words wisely.

What do I want to achieve through speaking? I want my daughter to see that I am willing to stand by my belief that the pen can be mightier than the sword. I want to repair the ideal that the expression of her truth in words, whether they be written or spoken, is a great power. I want her teacher to be commended for the work she does in promoting meaningful literacy. I want to raise questions that lead to dialogue that lead to change. I want to quiet my soul.

I am ready to speak. I approach the microphone. I see their nameplates. I feel the heat generating. I state my name. Their heads dart up. I see their faces. They know who I am. I ask the Blessed Mother to wrap Her light around the changing fabric of my words. I speak for fifteen minutes.

I ask that the record state that I am willing to volunteer my time and expertise to begin a newsletter in our district where the children can experience the power of the pen—a newsletter that weaves the voices of the children and elders in a dialogue that creates plain and luxurious patterns of change.

At the break I get up to leave. A woman puts her hand on my shoulder and whispers in my ear, "Your words were radiant." I feel too shy to say anything but thank you. I go to my car. I don't fight the tears. The different weaves of my experience integrate and I am home in the resting place of my soul.

Completion

No one from the Board of Education ever contacted me about my offer to begin a newsletter. No commendation from the Board of Education was ever made to Emma's teacher. No interest ever emerged on the part of my daughter to write another letter to the Board of Education.

I could keep this weave going forever.

I choose to call it complete.

I don't like the loose ends of this cloth. I know I need to accept that the fabric of letting go is messy.

I let the karmic stitches dissolve and throw the cloth over my shoulder. I ride into the world warmed by the weight of the published word.

The Spirit of 1776

4th of July. Barbeque at my brother's house. Time to go home. Four kids buckled in, we're loading the van.

Emma, our oldest, six-and-a-half years, sits next to Mary, our youngest, three-and-a half-months.

A lightening bug crawls on Mary's car seat. Emma thinks it's a bee. She screams, "Mom, Dad! There's a bee on Mary's car seat!"

We're trying to fold the double stroller.

Emma panics. "A bee, it's on Mary's face!"

We stop. "What?"

Lee sees the harmless bug crawling across Mary's smiling face.

Emma's face is frozen with terror. In an instant, with eyes closed, she grabs what she thinks is a bee and throws it out the open door of the van, screaming the whole time from the depths of her Warrior Heart.

She opens her eyes. The bee is gone. She checks to see that Mary is okay, Then she cries.

I take a deep breath and very deliberately place the moment I just witnessed into my heart. I hear Emma's dad comforting her "You're okay sweetheart. It was just a lightening bug. Mary is fine."

I take Emma in my arms. "What you did was very brave. You really are a hero."

She stops crying and says, "No I'm not. It was just a lightening bug."

"But you didn't know that."

"So what. A hero is someone who saves someone else's life."

I explain, "You're a hero because you let your love for Mary tell you what to do. You didn't let your scared feelings stop you from helping her. That's the kind of spirit that can change the world."

Weave of the Future

I hold the vision that one day
A cloth weaved from the sacred threads
Will wrap itself around our
Overworked and under appreciated
Mother Earth.
I see Her being able to finally rest and regenerate
Beneath the comforter of love and wisdom.
I see Her dreams returning to the realm
Where the beauty of evolution can be felt.
I see Her vibrational field being washed
By the Golden Light of God.

I am being summoned back to my workstation.
For now, the pause is complete.
Coffee cups emptied,
Phone calls finished,
Toilets flushed,
Hands washed,
Chocolate put back in the freezer,
I return to my children.
I take my place beside every mother
And every loved one who supports a mother's quest.
Together we get back to the enduring task
Of changing the fabric of the world
One thread at a time.

I am here for the long run.

Epilogue

As I prepared this book for publication, I found myself thinking a lot about whether or not to include the story "Weaving Between." I was hesitant because I talk about the West Babylon Board of Education and their dismissive attitude toward the naïve ideals of my eight-year-old daughter. I figured they would not like it and I have no basis to trust that their response would be beneficial to my family or community. Even as I struggled with this anxiety, I knew I had to take a leap of faith and trust that I could handle the outcomes of speaking my truth because it happens to be an important truth to speak out about.

When I was in the seventh grade, racial integration came to the schools of Brooklyn. 1975. My mother was President of the PTA and caught in the middle of a heated community battle. I watched her stand up at a meeting packed with 400 people. I watched the people scream, "Keep the Blacks out of our schools!!" I watched my mother find her voice as she nervously leaned into the microphone and stated, "I'm not neutral in this matter. I stand on the side of children and I will stand in front of this school as the buses arrive. I will welcome every one of those children to Seth Low Junior High School, not because they are Black but because they have a right to a good education."

I watched as the wiseguys of Bensonhurst came up to my mother and quietly threatened her safety if she continued to support the bussing in of the Marlboro Project kids. I watched as my father stepped up, pointed his two fingers directly into the eyes of the main thug and commanded in his thick Italian accent, "You don't tell my wife *anything*! You don't want to see those kids come to this school? Then I will do you a favor and *blind you*! Poke both your eyes out. Right now!" I watched as those men backed off and out of the auditorium.

I have spent much of my life watching the struggles of right and wrong and positioning myself in a way to understand all perspectives. I have considered my difficulty in choosing sides a weakness of character. I now understand that truth is not black or white. It moves between the two, generating light from the hidden places of connection. What I know to be true today may not be true tomorrow and with that in mind I can fix the silence of segregated thought and speak. I have always known that silence can be golden. Now I know that silence can also be deadly.

Once I made the decision to go forth with "Weaving Between," I returned to the senior citizen center in Wyandanch to get permission from John Newton to tell his story. When I arrived I met with the activities coordinator who originally arranged our interview with John and told her about my book.

I asked her, "Do you think John would want his story told?"

She answered, "Absolutely. He waited his whole life to have his story heard."

"Is he here today?"

"No."

"Can you give him an authorization to sign for me?"

"He died in August."

"Died?"

"Yeah. He was my buddy."

"He seemed so healthy."

"He was depressed, never got over it."

"He killed himself?"

"Shot himself."

"Does he have family?"

"None to speak of."

"What should I do?"

"Tell his story. Maybe it will finally give him peace."

I left the Center and I cried. I cried, and cried, and cried until all the fears I'd had about putting this book into the world washed away.

I speak now for all the children who do not have the words yet to express the pain they feel when they are dismissed at a moment when their hearts are full of hope. The nature of that kind of dismissal kills their innocence, leaving a tombstone of anger in the graveyard of their soul.

If only that bus driver had made a different choice, a choice guided by his compassion for a little boy standing on the corner in the rain, then a seed of hope might have been planted in the garden of John Newton's soul. The bloom of that one flower, that solitary rose, could have made all the difference.

How many opportunities do we have in a day, a week, a month, a year, a lifetime, to make the knowing choice? The choice that is guided by the mind, the heart, the soul.

The choice that does not obey the dogma of right and wrong, but rather bows down to the mysteries of love and truth.

I leave you with this: We each hold within our soul a voice that can be golden or deadly.

Please take care to govern the power of your words and deeds in the everyday little ways.

And trust the truth.

Thank you for reading my book.

About the Author

A creative-arts therapist, Marianne Chasen has been working with women, children and families for over 15 years. She attended Oxford and NYU, and is a state certified teacher in New York. Marianne is co-founder and director of Kid Esteem, Inc., a nonprofit organization based in Babylon, NY, dedicated to the emotional health and vitality of children, families and communities. She is married and the proud mother of four children.

For more information about Sacred Weave of Mothering Workshops, the author may be reached at: (631) 321-6675 or email: kidesteem@aol.com

PUBLISHING

Our Mission

Aslan Publishing offers readers a window to the soul via well-crafted and practical self-help books, inspirational books, and modern day parables. Our mission is to publish books that uplift one's mind, body, and spirit.

Living one's spirituality in business, relationships, and personal growth is the underlying purpose of our publishing company, and the meaning behind our name Aslan Publishing. We see the word "Aslan" as a metaphor for living spiritually in a physical world.

Aslan means "lion" in several Middle Eastern languages. The most famous "Aslan" is a lion inThe Chronicles of Narnia by C. S. Lewis. In these stories, Aslan is the Messiah, the One who appears at critical points in the story in order to point human beings in the right direction. Aslan doesn't preach, he acts. His actions are an inherent expression of who he is.

We hope to point the way toward joyful, satisfying and healthy relationships with oneself and with others. Our purpose is to make a real difference in our readers' everyday lives.

Titles Published by Aslan

The Candida Control Cookbook What You Should Know And What You Should Eat To Manage Yeast Infections
by Gail Burton
$14.95
ISBN 0-944031-67-6

Workout for the Soul: 8 Steps to Inner Fitness
by Chrissie Blaze
$14.95
ISBN 0-944031-90-0

The Gift of Wounding: Finding Hope & Heart in Challenging Circumstances
by Andre Auw Ph.D.
$13.95
ISBN 0-944031-79-X

How Loving Couples Fight: 12 Essential Tools for Working Through the Hurt
by James L Creighton Ph.D.
$16.95
ISBN 0-944031-71-4

Intuition Workout: A Practical Guide To Discovering & Developing Your Inner Knowing
by Nancy Rosanoff
$12.95
ISBN 0-944031-14-5

The Joyful Child: A Sourcebook of Activities and Ideas for Releasing Children's Natural Joy
by Peggy Jenkins Ph.D.
$16.95
ISBN 0-944031-66-8

More →

*Lovers For Life: Creating
Lasting Passion, Trust
and True Partnership*
by Daniel Ellenberg Ph.D.
& Judith Bell M.S., MFCC
$16.95
ISBN 0-944031-61-7

*Magnificent Addiction:
Discovering Addiction as
Gateway to Healing*
by Philip R. Kavanaugh, M.D.
$14.95
ISBN 0-944031-36-6

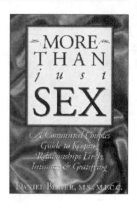

*More Than Just Sex:
A Committed Couples
Guide to Keeping
Relationships Lively,
Intimate & Gratifying*
by Daniel Beaver M.S., MFCC
$12.95
ISBN0-944031-35-8

*Mind, Music & Imagery:
Unlocking the Treasures
of Your Mind*
by Stephanie Merritt
$13.95
ISBN 0-944031-62-5

*New Woman Manager: 50
Fast & Savvy Solutions for
Executive Excellence*
by Sharon Lamhut Willen
$14.95
ISBN 0-944031-11-0

*The Motion Picture
Pre-scription Watch This
Movie and Call Me in The
Morning: 200 Movies to help
you heal life's problems*
by Gary Solomon Ph.D.
"The Movie Doctor "
$12.95
ISBN 0-944031-27-7

Solstice Evergreen: The History, Folklore & Origins of the Christmas Tree
2nd ed by Sheryl Karas
$14.95
ISBN 0-944031-75-7

What Happened to the Prince I Married: Spiritual Healing for a Wounded Relationship
by Sirah Vettese Ph.D.
$14.95
ISBN 0-944031-76-5

If You Want to be Rich & Happy Don't Go to School: Ensuring Lifetime Security for Yourself & Your Children
by Robert T. Kiyosaki
$15.95
ISBN 0-944031-59-5

More Aslan Titles

Facing Death, Finding Love: The Healing Power Of Grief & Loss in One Family's Life
by Dawson Church, $10.95; ISBN 0-944031-31-5

Gentle Roads to Survival: Making Self-Healing Choices in Difficult Circumstances
by Andre Auw Ph.D. $10.95; ISBN 0-944031-18-8

Lynn Andrews in Conversation with Michael Toms
edited by Hal Zina Bennett, $8.95; ISBN 0-944031-42-0

Argument With An Angel
by Jan Cooper, $11.95; ISBN 0-944031-63-3

To order any of Aslan's titles send a check or money order for the price of the book plus Shipping & Handling

Book Rate $3 for 1st book.; $1.00 for each additional book
First Class $4 for 1st book; $1.50 for each additional book

Send to: **Aslan Publishing**
2490 Black Rock Turnpike # 342
Fairfield CT 06825

To receive a current catalog: please call (800) 786–5427 or (203) 372–0300
E-mail us at: **info@aslanpublishing.com**
Visit our website at **www.aslanpublishing.com**

Our authors are available for seminars, workshops, and lectures. For further information or to reach a specific author, please call or email Aslan Publishing.

More →

SING
& CHANGE
THE WORLD!

From Davy Crockett
to Princess Di
Dozens of Voices
Show You How

by David Edward Dayton

Singing/Folklore • US $16.95 Canada $25.50

"Isn't it wonderful when a book comes along that can brighten up our lives? Sing & Change the World! by David Dayton is such a book. It not only offers great hope and inspiration, it creates a song in our hearts to help us deal with all of life's woes." –Bud Gardner, Co-Author "Chicken Soup for the Writer's Soul"

You don't have to be an Italian tenor to shake the rafters or shake up the status quo. With a little courage, a touch of whimsy and David Dayton as your guide, you'll soon discover how singing can change your life, and help you change the world.

Sing & Change the World! combines historic facts, in easily digestible form, with chicken-soup inspiration and Mozart-effect musical power to demonstrate the impact of singing on ordinary life. Singing has saved lives, freed slaves and stopped a world war. Historic characters, modern celebrities and everyday people have changed themselves and their world with a well-timed tune.

Sing & Change the World! will show you how to:
- **sing & save a life**
- **sing & find success**
- **sing & promote healing**
- **sing & change your mood**
- **sing & solve problems**
- **sing & change the world**

"informative, inspiring, well-researched, well-written—a delightful book. It is a must for every teacher's curriculum library." Betty Sturgess; Choir Director; Teacher of the Year; Writer of children's musicals

"An inspiring collection of anecdotes from a gifted teacher and self-taught musician who integrates music into every part of his classroom and life." – Dr. Dennis Mah, Charter School Director

Author, historian, kindergarten teacher David Dayton loves to sing, teach and spend time with his family. They sang while posing for this photo.

ISBN: 0 944031-92-7 **More →**